Daniel L Scott-Browne

Scott-Browne's Text-Book of Phonography ..

Part I.

Daniel L Scott-Browne

Scott-Browne's Text-Book of Phonography ..
Part I.

ISBN/EAN: 9783337140922

Printed in Europe, USA, Canada, Australia, Japan

Cover: Foto ©Andreas Hilbeck / pixelio.de

More available books at **www.hansebooks.com**

SCOTT-BROWNE'S
TEXT-BOOK of PHONOGRAPHY.

A NEW PRESENTATION OF THE PRINCIPLES OF
THE ART,

AS PRACTISED BY NINE-TENTHS OF THE MEMBERS OF THE PROFESSION IN AMERICA; AND THE ONLY WORK EMBODYING THE IMPROVEMENTS MADE IN THE LAST TEN YEARS.

FOR
SCHOOLS, COLLEGES AND PRIVATE INSTRUCTION.

BY
D. L. SCOTT-BROWNE.

TEACHERS OF THE ART FOR EIGHT YEARS IN THE COLLEGE OF PHONOGRAPHY; EDITOR OF "BROWNE'S PHONOGRAPHIC MONTHLY AND REPORTERS' JOURNAL" (ORGAN OF THE PROFESSION); AUTHOR OF THE AMERICAN STANDARD SERIES OF PHONOGRAPHIC TEXT-BOOKS; MEMBER OF THE AMERICAN PHILOLOGICAL SOCIETY.

PART I.

SEVENTH EDITION—REVISED.

NEW-YORK:
D. L. SCOTT-BROWNE,
1886.

COPYRIGHT BY
D. L. SCOTT-BROWNE,
1886.

PREFACE TO THE SEVENTH EDITION.

This work, presenting what is known as the AMERICAN STANDARD system of Phonography, contains the improvements made by the profession during the past twenty-five years' practice, down to date. It has become the leading text-book of phonography in the schools thruout the country where shorthand is taught, and, especially, in the Chain of Phonographic Colleges established by the author in the United States and elsewhere.

The chief improvements of this edition are: Better practise exercises on the upward and downward L and R, with simplified directions for understanding the application of these principles. Exercises in other parts of the work have been improved to make more positive and clear the application of such principles as might be employed in different ways, but which would be better used in one uniform manner, thus avoiding confusion in their application. The various lists of abbreviations have been supplied with practise exercises which aid to their easy mastery. Some writing exercises have been made over, supplying words better suited to clearly illustrate principles. The *Sen* principle, which by accident was omitted from the last three editions, has been added. Also directions for the formation of imperfect hooks or offsets, which have been difficult for the student to understand and which are now made clear. The affix signs have been better arranged. A list of about one hundred and fifty abbreviations added and general directions given for further study. Typographical and other discrepancies have been removed.

The book has been thoroly criticized by the author and teachers in general during its past four years' use, and being revised now for the third time, it is believed to be the best instruction book on shorthand writing. It has cost the author fifteen years' labor to bring the art to its present state of perfection and to present it in the most practicable manner, affording a book that will meet and remove the difficulties experienced by students.

The work presents but one style of writing equally suited to all uses required either by the amanuensis or verbatim reporter, and is in every respect the system receiving the highest acknowledgements of the profession and of teachers. THE AUTHOR.

Phonographic Headquarters,
   23 Clinton Place, New-York City.
Jan. 1886.

CONTENTS.

PREFACE	iii
TO THE LEARNER	v
DEFINITIONS	viii

CONSONANTS:—

Lesson I.—Consonant Alfabet	1

VOWELS AND VOWELIZATION:—

Lesson II.—Positiv and Relativ Values	6
Lesson III.—Short Vowels	13
Lesson IV.—Extra Vowels	17
Punctuation, Capitals, Emphasis	18
Lesson V.—Difthongs or Compound Vowels	19
Lesson VI.—Joined Vowel Ticks	21

CIRCLES AND LOOPS:—

Lesson VII.—Brief additional signs for *s* and *s*	22
Lesson VIII.—Loops for *st* and *str*	27

SEMICIRCLES AND HOOK:—

Lesson IX.—Brief Signs for *Wa* and *Ya*	29
Lesson X.—Brief *Wa* and *Ya* Signs disjoined	32

ASPIRATE TICK, HEH:—

Lesson XI.—Heh on stems	37

ABBREVIATIONS AND POSITION:—

Lesson XII.—Abbreviations—Simple and Compound Stems	38
Lesson XIII.—Abbreviations—Circles, Loops and Vowels	43
Lesson XIV.—Abbreviations—Brief *Wa* and *Ya* Signs—Vowel, Stem, and Brief Sign Combination	46

HALF-LENGTHS AND ED TICK:—

Lesson XV.—Halving Stems to add *t* or *d*—*ed* tick—Abbreviations	48

INITIAL HOOKS:—

Lesson XVI.—Small Initial Hooks for *l* and *r* on mated stems—*l* and *r* on unmated stems—Abbreviations	55
Lesson XVII.—The Initial Circle on *l* and *r* hook signs—Abbreviations	63
Lesson XVIII—Back Hook for *in, en, un*	66
Lesson XIX.—W-tick	67
Lesson XX.—Small Terminal Hooks for *n f* and *v*—Abbreviations	69
Expression of Numbers. (See Part II., page 144.)	
Lesson XXI.—*Shun* and *Eshun* Hooks—Abbreviations	75

SHADING AND LENGTHENING:—

Lesson XXII.—Shading *Em*—lengthening *ing*—lengthening other curves and *Ra* and *Hah*—Abbreviations	78

PREFIXES AND AFFIXES:—

Lesson XXIII.—Prefixes—Compound Prefixes	81
Lesson XXIV.—Affixes—Abbreviations as Affixes	85

TO THE LEARNER.

In taking up the study of Fonografy the learner must understand, from the start, that he is to lay aside the methods of both spelling and writing words as taught in our books and dictionaries; and that he must place himself in the attitude of a child who is just beginning to learn his A B C. There are two reasons for this advice:

1st.—The fonografik alfabet, unlike the one in our spelling books, contains as many letters or signs as there are elements or sounds in the English language, and not one of these letters or signs stands for more than one sound or value, hence, every word is to be spelled by just those letters or signs that represent the sound heard in the word—*one* sign for each sound, and no more. For example, the word *talk* is composed of *three* sounds, or elements, *t-aw-k*; *speak* is composed of four elements, *s-p-e-k*; *back*, three elements, *b-ă-k*; *laugh*, three elements, *l-ah-f*; etc. So, in fonografy, there must be just as many signs used in spelling a word as there are elements, or sounds, heard in the pronunciation of the word; *three* signs in spelling *talk*, because there are but *three* elements heard; *four* signs in *speak*, because there are but *four* elements heard; and so on, in this way with all the words in the language.

2d.—The letters or signs of the fonografik alfabet are all *new* and unfamiliar to the learner, the same as *a b c* are new and unfamiliar to the child just learning them, and must be acquired in the same way—by memorizing. The child memorizes principally by the *repeating* process. The adult shortens this process by bringing his mind—his judgment—his reasoning powers—to his assistance. He calls to his aid all the ideas that he can associate in any way with the lessons he is learning, that could avail him any thing in acquiring them. The more intelligent the student, the more will he *learn by this law of association of ideas.*

The quickest way to learn the alfabet is, First: read it over, noticing the *name, sound, form, direction* and *thickness* or *shading* of each sign. Second: **read carefully** what is said about the *manner of writing* the stems—whether upward or downward, etc., following the directions given in the Text-Book, on page 2. Third: write the first eight stems of the alphabet, making and naming them in pairs, accenting the second one of each pair, and repeating words to rhyme with them as follows:

Pe *Be,* Te *De,* Cha *Ja,* Ka *Ga;*
This *is* for *me* to *learn* this *day.*

Also notice that the stems are arranged in the same regular order as the spokes of a wheel, and that there is a *thin* and *thick* or *light* and *heavy* spoke to each direction, thus: which, paired thus: and separated without breaking their order, appear just as they are seen in the alfabet:

Pe *Be,* Te *De,* Cha *Ja,* Ka *Ga.*
This *is* for *me* to *learn* this *day.*

Then write the next eight stems, making and naming them also in pairs, and repeating words that will rhyme with them:

Ef *Ve,* Ith *The,* Es *Ze,* Ish *Zhe;*
This *too,* for *me* to *learn,* you *see.*

The remaining stems are unmated and divided into triplets, with words to rhyme, as follows:

La Er *Ra,* Em Un *Ing;*
Did you *say* I might *sing?*
Wa Ya Hah.
Yes, ha-*ha!*

Write the alfabet in SCOTT-BROWNE'S FONOGRAFIK COPY BOOK, following the directions therein given. The last alfabet exercise in the Copy-Book being like the one on page 3 of this book. If the Copy-Book is not used, any blank note-book will do, taking care to have the exercises neatly and correctly written.

At this point ask *why* some of the stems are mated—differing only in being *light* and *heavy.* Answer. Because the elements or sounds represented by the stems of each mated pair are formed alike in the mouth, and *are* alike, with the exception that the light ones, *p, t,* etc., are *whispered,* while their mates or cognates, *b, d,* etc., are *voiced*—the voice being heard before the lips separate to give them utterance. Therefore the *whispered* mated elements are represented by light lines—light *sound,* light *stem*—and the *voiced* mated elements by *heavy* lines—heavy *sound,* heavy *stem.* Pronouncing the syllables *ap, ab; at, ad; ach, aj; ak, ag;* etc., will enable the student to preceive, at once, both the similarity and difference between the mated elements.

The unmated elements are all voiced except *Hah,* and are represented by the curved stems that remained after the mated stems were provided for.

PENS AND PENCILS.

Practise with either pen or pencil. It is better to be familiar with the use of both. Let the pen be fine, and the ink clear and black. Hold the pen loosely so that it can be turned easily in writing the outlines of words containing stems made in different directions. Some reporters hold the pen or pencil between the first and second fingers. It is a good way, as the pen is more easily controlled and it enables one to write longer without fatigue. Both this and the usual way are recommended—each as a rest to the other. Of pencils graded by numbers, use No. 3; of Dixon's pencils, use those marked S. M. (Soft Medium); of the American Fonografic Pencils, use those marked S (Soft).

TIME REQUIRED TO LEARN PHONOGRAPHY.

Directions faithfully followed and lessons thoroughly learned, together with an hour's daily practise, will enable the average student to master this book in about two months. A month's additional practise, of from two to three hours daily, from another's reading—using any common school reading books (from Second to Fourth—omitting all the poetry), and good business letters—will fit the student to begin the work of receiving dictations of business letters, provided he can *spell*, *punctuate* and *write* longhand, or operate a writing machine well. These three are positiv pre-requisites in a shorthand amanuensis.

HOW AND WHEN TO PRACTISE.

In writing after another's reading let the same matter be repeated three times, at least. This enables the writer to criticise his first effort, make corrections, choose better forms for words, and improve generally the appearance of the second effort. The third effort confirms the corrections and improvements of the second and advances one's speed. After writing any thing the third time let the shorthand notes be *read* as many as two or three times and written out in longhand *once*. Repetition in writing and reading practise, is one of the secrets of gaining speed in writing and readiness in reading. As progress is made in correctness and speed of writing, the repeating practice can be gradually discontinued. Let the student *always* read every thing he writes. One's own notes, after becoming able to write easily, make better reading exercises than engraved fonografy. Amanuenses and reporters will have no trouble in reading their notes if, during the preparatory course, they faithfully read every thing they write.

DEFINITION OF FONOGRAFY, ETC.

FONOGRAFY (Phonography).—Any system of writing language in which only *the* SOUNDS *of the* SPOKEN *word are represented.*

STENOGRAFY.—Any system of shorthand writing, using brief alfabetic signs, arbitrary characters, principles of contraction, etc., adequate to the representation and speed of **verbatim speech. The term** is applied to systems of un-fonetik shorthand.

STENO-FONOGRAFY.—**Any** system of fonetic shorthand employing **the** alfabetik signs **of** stenography, principles of abbreviation **and** contraction, devices, etc., adequate to **the** representation and **speed** of verbatim speech.

FONETIKS (Phonetics).—The science **of the sounds of the human** voice.—(Webster.)

FONETIK (Phonetic) or **Fonik** (Phonic).—Relating to the representation of sounds by characters.—(Webster.)

Fonetik or *Fonik Shorthand* and *Steno-Fonografy* both mean one and the same thing.

The system of Shorthand or Stenografy taught in this book is fonetik or fonografik, and, **hence, like all** other systems having a fonetik basis, **is** termed, for brevity, *Fonografy* instead of *Steno-Fonografy*, there being no longhand fonografy to require the other as a distinguishing name.

PRONUNCIATION OF NATURE, QUESTION, ETC.

The theoretical pronunciation of the words *nature, future,* **question,** *fixture,* etc., is not so conveniently or quickly represented in fonografy as the popular pronunciation; therefore this **work** sanctions the fonografik writing of **nachur, fuchur, queschun,** *fixchur,* etc. If the reporter is to write what he *hears,* he will seldom have occasion to represent other than the popular pronunciation given to this class of words.

LESSON I.

1.—CONSONANT ALFABET.

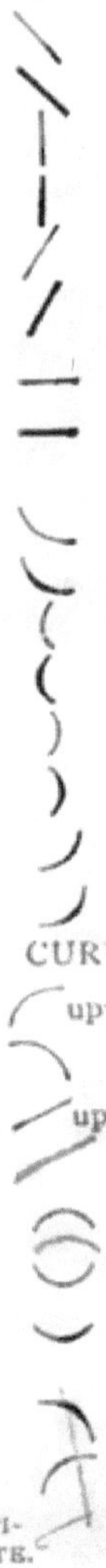

	Fonografik Stem or Letter.	Name.	Sound.	Power.
				STRAIGHT STEMS (Mated).
ABRUPT ELEMENTS.		Pe	p	as in .... u*p*
		Be	b	,, ... a*b*
		Te	t	,, ... i*t*
		De	d	,, ... ai*d*
		Cha	ch	,, ... ea*ch*
		Ja	j	,, ... *j*oy, a*g*e, e*dg*e
		Ka	k	,, ... oa*k*, *c*oo, e*ch*o
		Ga	g	,, ...e*gg*, e*g*o
				CURVED STEMS (Mated).
CONTINUANT ELEMENTS.		Ef	f	as in .... i*f*, lau*gh*, *ph*ase
		Ve	v	,, ... e*v*e, Ste*ph*en
		Ith	th	,, ... oa*th*
		The	dh	,, ... *th*e
		Es	s	,, ... u*s*, a*c*e
		Ze	z	,, ... oo*z*e, a*s*
		Ish	sh	,, ... a*sh*, o*c*ean
		Zhe	zh	,, ... a*z*ure
				CURVED AND STRAIGHT STEMS (Not Mated).
LIQUID ELEMENTS.	upward	La	l	as in .... a*l*e
		Er	r	,, ... ea*r*
	upward	Ra	r	,, ... *r*oa*r*
NASAL ELEMENTS.		Em	m	,, ... ai*m*
		Un	n	,, ... a*n*
		Ing	ng	,, ... so*ng*
COALESCENT ELEMENTS.		Wa	w	,, ... *w*ay
		Ya	y	,, ... *y*ou
ASPIRATE.	upward	Hah	h	,, ... *h*ay

MANNER OF WRITING THE STEMS.

2. The Stems ＼ *Pe,* ＼ *Be,* | *Te,* | *De,* ／ *Cha,* ／ *Ja,* are written *downward.*

3. ── *Ka,* ── *Ga,* are written from *left* to *right.*

4. ＼ *Ef,* ＼ *Ve,* (*Ith,* (*The,*) *Es,*) *Ze,* ⌡ *Zh!,* are written *downward.*

5. ⌡ *Ish* is written downward when it is the only stem in a word, but when joined to other stems may be written either *upward* or *downward,* according to rules given in advanced lessons. When written upward it is named *Sha.*

6. ⌠ *La* is written upward when it is the only stem in a word, but when joined to other stems may be written either *upward* or *downward,* according to rules given in advanced lessons. When written downward it is named *El.*

7. ⌐ *Er* is always written *downward.*

8. ／ *Ra* is always written *upward.*

9. ⌒ *Em,* ⌣ *Un,* ⌣ *Ing,* are written from *left* to *right.*

10. ⌐ *Wa,* ⌠ *Ya,* are written *downward.*

11. ⌐ *Hah* is always written **upward.**

RESUMÉ.

a. ⌡ *Ish,* written *downward* when it is the only stem in a word. Written either *upward* or *downward,* according to certain rules, when joined to other stems. *Upward* name, *Sha.*

b. ⌠ *La,* written *upward* when it is the only stem in a word. Written either *upward* or *downward,* according to certain rules, when joined to other stems. *Downward* name, *El.*

c. ／ *Ra,* ⌿ *Hah,* always written *upward.*

d. ── *Ka,* ── *Ga,* ⌒ *Em,* ⌣ *Un,* ⌣ *Ing,* written from *left* to *right.*

e. All the other stems invariably **written *downward.***

NOTE.—Trace and name every one of the stems on page 1 several times; after which, practise writing them in "Scott-Browne's Phonographic Copy-Book," page 1.

12.—EXERCISE TO BE WRITTEN IN COPY-BOOK.

Pe, Be,
Te, De,
Cha, Ja,
Ka, Ga,
Ef, Ve,
Ith, The,
Es, Ze,
Ish, Zhe,
La *or* El,
Er,
Ra,
Em,
Un,
Ing,
Wa,
Ya,
Hah.

NOTE.—For practise on this exercise see page 2 of "Phonographic Copy-Book."

MANNER OF JOINING CONSONANT STEMS.

13. When two **or more stems are** used in the outline of a word, they are written without lifting the pen; the next beginning where the preceding one ends. Illustration:

p k,   n t,   r m l,   b n t,   r r,   k k,   m m,   m n.

14. RULE I.—The *first downward* stem of a consonant outline must *end* on the line of writing. Illustration:

k p,   f v,   ch k,   p p,   n l,   d t.

15. RULE II.—The *first upward* stem of a consonant outline must *begin* on the line of writing. Illustration:

r k,   l l,   h n,   sh l,   m r.

16. Join the following stems without making an angle:

l k,   p n,   th n,   l n,   v g,   d f,   l r,

l s,   m s,   m n,   m ng,   b ng,   t n,   r sh.

17. Always make an angle between the following stems:

f n,   v ng,   l m,

18. Curve *Em* a little more before *Ka* and a little less before *Te*, in order to secure sharper angles; thus: *m k,   m t.*

Practise on the foregoing outlines until they can be written readily and neatly.

Read carefully and with patience, the Exercise on the following page, pronouncing aloud, first the *name*, and then the *sound* of each stem. Illustration:

NAMES.   SOUNDS.

Pe-Em   p m, sounding the *p* as in *ape,* leaving off the *a;* m as in *me,* leaving off *e.*

NOTE.—For practise on this exercise **see page 3 of** "Phonographic Copy-Book"

19.—READING EXERCISE.

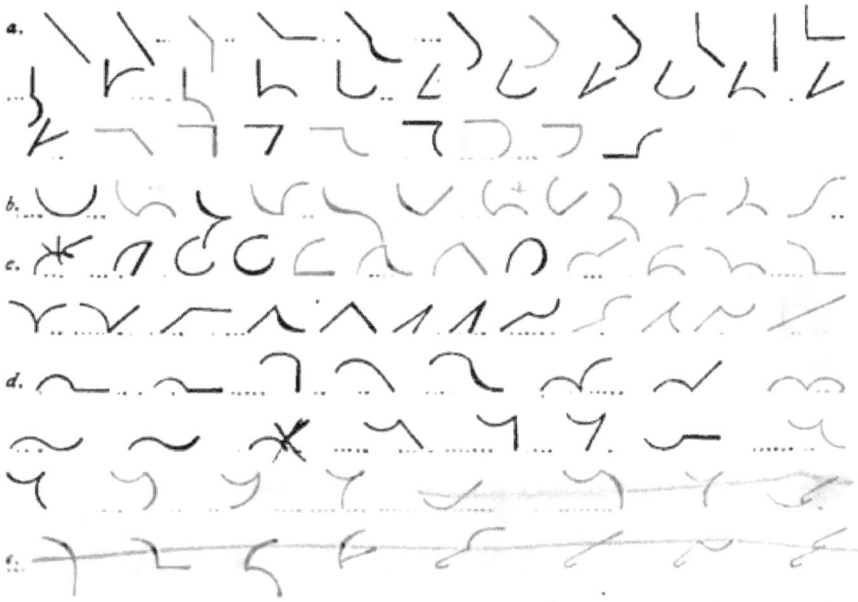

20. The hook on *Hah* cannot be made perfectly when *Hah* is joined to *Ja*, *Ya*, etc., but an imperfect hook or *offset* is made on the stems, which is just as legible to the student as the complete hook, after becoming familiar with it.

The above Reading Exercise contains the correct consonant outlines of the following words:

21.—WRITING EXERCISE.

a. Pope, pub, pity, pick; bevy, busy, bush, bijou; Tobby, tidy, tag; daisy, duly, door, dame, deny; check, China, cherry; Johnny, gem, jury, Jehu; keep, Cady, cage, coffee; Goth, Gussie, gush, gaily.

b. Fish, fame; vale, valley, veer, vary; theme, thorough; sewer; zeal; sham, shallow.

c. Lehigh, lodge, Lena, lung, league, love, lobby, Lizzie, Laura, Alma; arm, ark, early, Aurora; rock, review, rib, rich, ridge, rash, rely, wreath, renew, rear.

d. Make, mug, meadow, map, move, mail, Mary, maim, money, among, Mayhew; nap, into, inch, nag, enough, knoweth, noisy, Nash, nail, narrow, anyway, N. Y. (*En-Ya*), N. H. (*En-Hah*).

e. Await, awoke, Oyer, Yahoo; holy, Harry, honey, ha-ha.

NOTE.—Practise on pages 4 and 5 of "Scott-Browne's Phonographic Copy-Book."

VOWELS AND VOWELIZATION.
LESSON II.
POSITIV AND RELATIV VALUES.

1. The *sound* for which any sign or letter stands is called the *value* or *power* of that sign or letter; and if that sign or letter never stands for any other value or power—never changes its value, but always keeps the same—that value is termed *fixed*, or *positiv*, or *absolute*,—all three of these words being in use to express the same idea. It has been observed in the foregoing lesson that the values of the fonografik (phonographic) consonant-signs are positiv, fixed, unchanging; that is, p is always *p*, and d always *d*, wherever they are written, and never stand for the sound of *f* or *t* or any other value than each its own.

2. But in this lesson it will be noticed that the values of the *simple* vowel signs are not positiv, but are dependent upon their *relation to the consonant stem* for their values. To illustrate: A heavy dot written opposit the *beginning* of a stem thus, |, is called *e*, but if this same dot is moved down opposit the *middle* of the stem, thus, •|, it is called *a*, and if moved again down opposit the *end* of the stem, thus, .|, it is called *ah;* thus forming a short scale of three sounds, *e, a, ah,*—the consonant stem being of a convenient size to furnish three distinctly different vowel sounds. By this, then, it is seen that the *simple* vowel signs do not have *fixed* values, as it can not be known what to call a dot till it has been *placed* by the side of a stem; hence, it is said that the vowel signs possess *relativ* value; that is, their *relation* to the stem must be shown before it can be known what sound, or value, to giv them.

3. The vowel signs, then, possess *not positiv* but *relativ* value, and are represented by *dots* and *dashes* written in three different places by the side of the consonant stem, and made *heavy* and *light* to correspond with *long* and *short* vowel sounds. *Heavy* signs for *long* vowels and *light* signs for *short* ones.

THE VOWEL SCALE, OR ALFABET.

4. There are, in the English language, sixteen *simple* vowel elements—six long, and ten short,—and seven *compound* vowels, or difthongs, as heard in the following words:—

LONG VOWELS.

B*e*, *e*rr, f*a*re, f*a*r, f*a*ll, m*o*ve.

SHORT VOWELS.

*I*t, *e*ll, *u*p, c*u*r, *a*t, *a*sk, l*o*g, wh*o*le, w*o*lf, and i̯,*
the initial element of the difthong, i̯-*öö*, heard in the words *blue*, *rue*, *rude*, *tune*, *suit*, etc.

COMPOUND VOWELS, OR DIFTHONGS.

*A*le, *o*ld, *i*ce, *oi*l, *ow*l, tr*ue*, p*ure*.

5. For practical reporting purposes it is not found necessary to represent each of these elements with a distinct sign of its own. Eighteen signs are regarded sufficient—fourteen *simple* and four *compound* signs. Two of the seven difthongs—*a* and *o*—are, for reasons not necessary to explain here, classed, in fonografy (phonography), with the simple vowels and represented by simple signs.

LONG VOWELS AND THEIR SIGNS.

6. The six long vowels (including *a* and *o*), classed together, are as follows:

   e a ah aw o oo

and represented thus:

e	a	ah	aw	o	oo
W*e*	g*a*ve	*a*lms	*a*ll	c*o*ld	f*oo*d.

7. When a vowel sign is written opposit the *beginning* of a stem it is said to be in the *first place;* when opposit the *middle* of a stem, in the *second place;* when opposit the *end* of a stem, the *third place.*

8. Observe that the *beginning* or *first place*, of a vowel, is where the stem *begins to be written*. The *first place* of *Pe*, *Cha*, *Ef*, *Ith*, etc., is at the *top* because that is where those stems *begin*; while the *first place* of *La*, *Ra*, *Hah*, is at the *bottom*, because that is where those stems begin. (See next page, lines 2–7, first and fourth columns.)

9. The dash signs are written at right angles to the consonant stem; that is, in an *opposit direction* to that of the stem. (See next page, fourth, fifth and sixth columns.)

10. The consonant portion of a word is written first and the vowel portion afterwards.

---

* This sound is *formed* in the mouth like the vowel in *it*, but *uttered* like the vowel in *up*, from the *back* of the mouth, with the throat as nearly in position for sounding ŭ (in *up*) as the tongue can allow and preserve the *form* of I (in *it*).

11.—EXERCISE ON LONG VOWELS.

DOTS.			DASHES.		
BEGINNING.	MIDDLE.	END.	BEGINNING.	MIDDLE.	END.
1st place.	2nd place.	3rd place.	1st place.	2nd place.	3rd place.
W-*e*	g-*a*-ve	*a*-lms	*a*-ll	c-*o*-ld	f-*oo*-d
Te	ta	tah	taw	toe	too
Key	kay	kah	caw	coe	coo
(4)	(4)	(4)	(4)	(4)	(4)
(5)	(5)	(5)	(5)	(5)	(5)
(6)	(6)	(6)	(6)	(6)	(6)
(7)	(7)	(7)	(7)	(7)	(7)
Eat	ate	aht	awt	oat	oot
Eke	ache	ahk	awk	oak	ook
(10)	(10)	(10)	(10)	(10)	(10)
(11)	(11)	(11)	(11)	(11)	(11)
(12)	(12)	(12)	(12)	(12)	(12)

12. RULE III.—Vowels that are read *before* a consonant are written to the *left* of vertical and inclined stems, the same as they would be in longhand, and *above* horizontal stems, the same as an *upper line of writing* reads before a *lower line*. Illustration:

ope, aid, eve, oath, ace, ooze, eel, awl,

ore, eke, ache, oak, aim, e'en, own.

13. RULE IV.—Vowels that are read *after* a consonant are written to the *right* of vertical and inclined stems, and *below* horizontal stems. Illustration:

bow, tea, dough, fee, sow, shoe, law, ray, hah,

key, coo, gay, may, ma, knee, neigh, gnaw, know.

14. In naming the letters, or signs, of fonografik (phonographic) words, be careful to get the exact sound for each sign, and, after spelling the words by their correct sounds, be doubly careful to pronounce them exactly as they were spelled. Illustration:

a-p, *ape*, and not *ăp;*

t-a-m, *tame*, and not *tăm;*

d-o-m, *dome*, and not *dŏm;*

t-a-k, *take*, not *tack;*

b-a-k, *bake*, not *back;*

r-a-t, *rate*, not *rat*.

In this way, carefully spell, both by sound and name of each sign, and pronounce, **correctly,** the fonografik words on page 11.

15. Do not allow the common, printed spelling **to** mislead when spelling a word in fonografy. Illustration:

Ache, *ā-k*, and not *a-se-aitch-e;*

coo, *k-ōō*, and not *se-double-o;*

thaw, *Ith-aw*, not *te-aitch-a-doubleyou;*

eel, *e-l*, **not** *double-e-l;*

talk, *t-aw-k*, not *t-a-el-k;*

though, *The-o*, **not** *t-aitch-o-you-je-aitch;*

gale, *Ga-a-l*, not *je-a-l-e;*

shawl, *Ish-aw-l*, not *Es-aitch-a-doubleyou-l;*

rouge, *Ra-ōō-Zhe*, not *ar-o-you-je-e.*

cage, *k-a-j*, not *se-a-je e.*

16. Write no more signs in a word than there are sounds heard in its pronunciation. Silent letters seen in printed words are never represented in fonografy. Illustration: Know, *n-o* — ⋎; gnaw, *n-aw* — ⌒; see, *s-e* — ⌐; cope, *k-o-p* — ⌐.

17. Before writing a word in fonografy pronounce it slowly and then sound all the elements *separately*, heard in the slow pronunciation, **in order** to determine the *exact sounds*, and the *correct signs* to be written. Illustration:

Word.	Slow pronunciation.	Separate sounds.	Names of consonant stems.	Stem outline.	Name of each sound.	Full word
Zero,	z e r o,	z-e-r-o,	**Ze-Ra**	⋎	Ze-e-Ra-o	⋎
Dado,	d a d o,	d-a-d-o,	**De-De**	|	De-a-De-o	|
Cocoa,	c o c oa,	k-o-k-o,	Ka-Ka	——	Ka-o-Ka-o	——
Delay,	d e l ay,	d-e-l-a,	De-La	⌐	De-e-La-a	⌐

NOTE.—Remember that the pen must not be lifted till all the consonant stems of an outline are written, after which the vowel signs are placed.

18.—READING EXERCISE
ON LONG VOWELS.

1st Place Vowels.

2nd Place Vowels.

3rd Place Vowels.

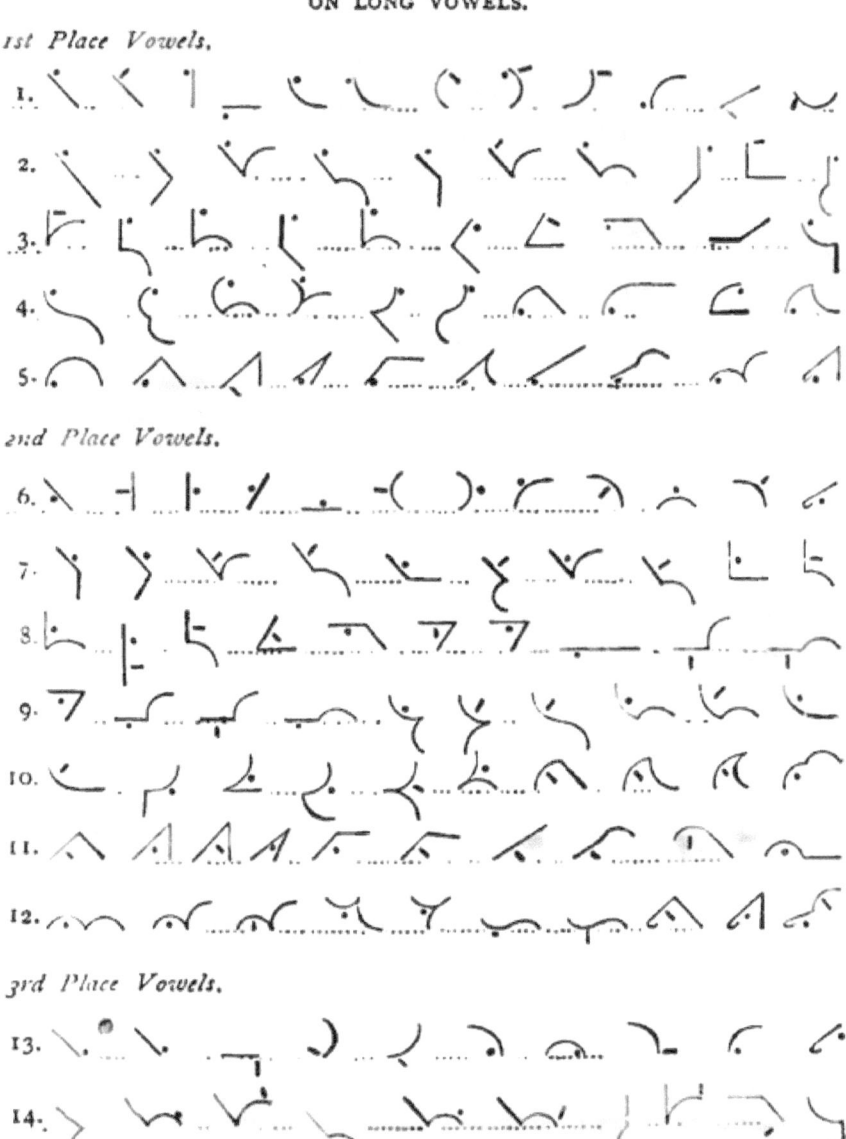

19.—WRITING EXERCISE

ON THE LONG VOWELS.

Pea, pa, paw, Po, poo, ape, ope, bay, baa, bow, obey, eat, ate, oat, tea, aid, ode, day, dough, age, Jo, eke, ache, oak, key, coo, gay, fee, fay, foe, eve, oath, thaw, sou, ace, ooze, Shah, shaw, show, shoe, lee, lay, lo, eel, ale, awl, aim, ma, knee, gnaw, woe, woo, yah, yo, haw, hoe, hah.

Peep, pope, peach, poach, peak, poke, opaque, Peko, peal, pail, pale, Paul, pole, babe, beat, beet, bait, boat, beach, beak, bake, bail, ball, bowl, below, beam, tape, teach, teeth, tail, tall, toll, team, tame, deep, daub, dado, dale, dole, delay, deem, dame, dome, cheap, cheat, Choate, cheek, chalk, choke, Job, joke, jail, keep, cape, cope, coach, cage, cake, coke, keel, coal, comb, gale, goal, game, feed, fade, Feejee, faith, fame, foam, veto, evoke, vague, vogue, thief, thieve, theme, sheep, shape, Shēik, shake, zeal, leap, lobe, load, leach, liege, leak, lake, leaf, loaf, leave, loathe, leal, lame, leeway, mope, meek, muck, meal, male, mail, mole, maim, knave, 'neath, name, heap, heat, hate, heed, hoed, heath, halo, ho-ho, ha-ha.

Write *Ra* for *r* in the following words, because it begins a -syllable:

Ray, raw, rōw, reap, rope, robe, rate, wrought, wrote, reed, raid, road, rowed, reach, rage, wreak, rake, rogue, wreath, wreathe, relay ream, roam, Rome, rear, roar, Reno, zero, Nero, hero.

Write *Er* for *r* in the following words, because it ends a syllable:

Ore, oar, pier, peer, pour, bier, bore, tēar, tore, deer, door, chore, jeer, fear, four, veer, shear, shore, leer, lore.

Write *El* (downward) for *l* in the following words, because it is final and preceded by either *f*, *v* or the upward *r*, in which case it must be written downward:

Fail, foal, veal, vale, reel, rail.

Write *Sha* and *La* (both upward) for *sh* and *l* in the following words, because they make the best joining:

Shawl, shoal, shield, leash.

LESSON III.

SHORT VOWELS.

1. The six short vowels, classed together, are **heard in the following syllables:**

    ĭ(t)   ĕ(t)   ă(t)   ŏ(t)   ŭ(t)   o͝o(t)

and are represented thus:

    ĭ   ĕ   ă   ŏ   ŭ   o͝o
    *I*t f*e*ll fl*a*t *o*n p*u*p's f*oo*t
                   *a*sk   c*u*r

2. The six *long* and six *short* vowels may be easily memorized by repeating the following words containing them:

    W*e* gave *a*lms—*a*ll c*o*ld f*oo*d.
    e   *a*   *a*   *ä*   *ō*   *ōō*
    *I*t f*e*ll fl*a*t—*o*n p*u*p's f*oo*t.
    it *et* *at* *ot* *ut* *oot*

3. Rules for writing vowels heard *between* STEM CONSONANTS:

RULE V.—ALL *first place* and the two long *second place* vowels, *a* and *o*, are written *after* the *first* consonant. Illustration:

    peak *big* *talk* *dock* *bake* *dome* *cake* *comb.*

RULE VI.—ALL the *third place* and the two SHORT *second place* vowels, *ĕ* and *ŭ*, are written *before* the *second* consonant. Illustration:

    palm *boom* *tack* *took* *neck* *numb*

NOTE.—If *first place* vowels were written *before* the *second* stem, and *third place* vowels *after* the *first* stem, it would bring the vowel signs within the angles, and then it could not be told whether the vowel was a *first* place one to the *second* stem or a *third* place one to the *first* stem. Illustration: It cannot be told whether the first word is *balm* or *beam*, or the second word, *pack* or *pick*; but by applying Rule V. the following word, ◝, is known to be *beam*, and by applying Rule VI. this word, ◞, is known to be *balm*.

4. The second place **vowels** could be written to either stem, but to make an equal division of the signs to each stem it was thought best by Mr. Pitman to write the long ones to the *first* and the short ones to the *second* stem, which added to the legibility of such words as ◝ *bake*, ◝ *beck*, ◟ *dome*, ◟ *dumb*, etc., when in careless or rapid writing the size of the vowel was not accurate.

5.—READING EXERCISE
ON SHORT VOWELS.

1. ˈit   ˈet   ˌat   ˌot   −ut   −out
   It   fell   flat   on   pup's   hot.

1st Place Vowels.

2. [shorthand characters]
3. [shorthand characters]
4. [shorthand characters]
5. [shorthand characters]
6. [shorthand characters]

2nd Place Vowels.

7. [shorthand characters]
8. [shorthand characters]
9. [shorthand characters]
10. [shorthand characters]

3rd Place Vowels.

11.
12.
13.
14.

6.—WRITING EXERCISE
ON SHORT VOWELS.

Ebb, abby, odd, eddy, add, itch, etch, edge, echo, egg, ash, ill, ell, Ella, alley, Emma, Anna, pity, petty, patty, putty, pod, pitch, patch, pick, peck, pack, Puck, pig, pygmy, peg, pug, pith, pussy, push, pill, pull, pully, pink, batch, badge, budge, back, book, big, beg, bag, bog, bug, buggy, bevy, busy, bush, bushy, bijou, bill, billow, bell, ballét (ballay), bung, tip, tap, top, tub, attach, touch, tick, tack, attack, tuck, attic, tag, tug, taffy, tally, tarry, Tenney, tung, tank, dip, ditty, oddity, dig, dog, dug, death, doth, dell, dull, dally, doll, dim, dumb, ding, dong, chip, chap, chop, chat, chick, check, chill, chilly, chimney, chink, jib, job, jet, jut, Judd, judge, Jack, jockey, jig, jag, jog, jug, gill, jelly, jolly, gem, Jennie, Johnnie, Kipp, cab, cob, cub, Kitty, catch, cudgel, Cudjo, kick, cook, keg, cog, coffee, café, kith, cash, calla, callow, king, kink, gig, gag, Goth, gush, galley, gull, gully, gum, guinea, gang, gong, fob, fitch, fetch, fudge, fag, fog, foggy, fellow, fallow, follow, Fanny, funny, fang, valley, volley, vim, thatch, thick, thicket, thumb, thong, zinc, ship, shop, shabby, shadow, shock, shook, shaggy, sham, shank, lip, lap, lop, elbow, Libby, lobby, lad, laddie, ledge, allege, lodge, lick, lack, lock, locket, luck, lucky, look, live, love, lofty, loth, lilly, loll, lull, limb, lamb, rally, map, mop, mob, Mattie, meadow, match, mock, muck, mug, miff, muff, myth, moth, mash, mush, mashed, mill, milk, mellow, mum, mummy, Minnie, Moony, many, monk, nip, nap, knap, nib, knob, Netie, niche, notch, nudge, nick, neck, knack, knock, nook, knag, nag, gnash, unlucky, ninny, Nancy,

APPLICATION OF R STEMS.

The rules governing the uses of upward and downward R cannot be given till all the modifications of consonants have been presented. Chapter XII. of PART II. TEXT-BOOK treats of the r-stems in all their relations, the first part of which chapter would be helpful for the student to examine in this connection.

Observe the engravings thruout this book for the uses of upward and downward r, as the correct employment of these stems will preserve legibility in phonographic outlines.

Write Er, (downward r), in ending a syllable, thus: Ear, oar, o'er, ark, peer, par, fore, poor, tear, tore, fear, Ehrich.

Write Ra (upward r) when beginning a syllable, thus: (1.) Rock, rug, rack, rig, rip, rap, rot, rut, rib, red, rich, wretch, rook, ring, rim, rum, ram; (2) when terminating the consonant form of a word and followed by a vowel, thus; Perry, Parry, bury, berry, cherry, ferry, Ferrie; (3) when followed by f, v, th, dh. s, z, t, d, ch or j, thus: Roof, reeve, Orth, wreathe, urso, razee, art, arrayed, arch, ridge, (4) when r immediately follows k, g, m, th, or dh, thus: Coregeer, mar, theory, thoraic; (5) when r follows Ra or Hah, thus: Rear, roar, Harry, hurry, hero.

APPLICATION OF THE L STEM.

The rules governing the uses of upward and downward L cannot be given till all the modifications of consonant stems have been explained. Chapter XIII. of PART II. TEXT-BOOK treates the l-stem in all its relations, the sections of which chapter, referred to below, could be examined to advantage in this connection.

The upward and downward l, unlike the upward and downward r is not written in these ways so much for legibility as to favor speed of writing. The only place where illegibility or conflict could occur is where the first and second rules (below) are violated.

Write El (downward l) when preceded by a vowel and followed by k, g, or m, thus: (1). elk, alack, elect, Alleghany, alum, elm; (2.) When final, and immediately following f, v, th, l, Ra and h, thus: lull, rill, hill (see section 5 of page 66, Part II.); (3.) When preceded by n or ng, thus: Nellie, kingly, knell, (see section 3, page 65, Part II.); (4.) When followed by the consonant stems g, n, or ng, thus: log, lag, leg, Ilion, Olney, lung, Lang, lank.

La (upward l) is used in all other cases; see sections 2, 4 and 6 of Part II., Chapter XIII., and when Part I. is finished and that chapter reached in the study of Part II. it must be thoroly mastered.

LESSON IV.

EXTRA VOWELS
AND THEIR SIGNS.

1. The vowels *ê* in *her* and *â* in *dare* are not classed in their proper places with the other long vowels, partly on account of such an arrangement breaking up the usual six-vowel order of long and short vowels, and partly because some fonografik authors do not provide for their representation, but use as substitutes either the second place *light* dot *ĕ* for the sound of *e* in *her* and *i* in *sir* or the *light* dash *ŭ* for *u* in *cur*, and the second place *heavy* dot *a* for the vowel in *dare*. It is much better that these distinct sounds have distinct signs of their own, and this book provides proper representation for them as follows:

2. A light dash written in *second place*, parallel with the stem for the vowel in *her*, *sir*, etc., and in *third place*, parallel with the stem, for the vowel in *dare*. Illustration: ⟍ *err* ˥⁻ *Goethe* (Ge(r)tuh), ⟍ *air*, ⌣ *fairy*.

3. The vowel in *ask*, *past*, *alas*, etc., is the true short mate of the vowel in *far*, the correct sign for which is the *third place light dot* used also to represent the sharper vowel heard in *rat*, which is the short mate of the vowel heard in *air*, *dare*, etc. On account of the similarity of these two vowels it is not necessary, for reporting purposes, to have two distinct signs. Should a distinct sign be required, in order to teach exact pronunciation, the *light* third place parallel dash can be used to represent the short vowel in *rat*, and the same sign made heavy to represent the long vowel in *dare*.

4. The vowel heard in *cur*, *work*, *journey*, etc., is more of a guttura than the one heard in *earnest*, *mercy*, *girl*, etc., and is represented by the second place light dash, as in *cup*.

5.—READING EXERCISE
ON EXTRA VOWELS.

6.—WRITING EXERCISE.

ON EXTRA VOWELS.

Goethe, Percy, (*Ra* for *r*), mercy.

Write *Er* for *r* in the following **words**:

Herb, herbage, herbal, earl, **early**, ergo, air, airy, pair, pare, pear, bear, **bare**, barely, tare, dare, **Adair**, fare, fair, affair, lair.

Write *Ra* for *r* in the following words: Fairy, Thayer, rare, mare, rarer (three lengths of *Ra*), thus:

Fair day. Percy came early. Poor, cheap fare. **Rare, early** pear.

PUNCTUATION, CAPITALS, EMPHASIS.

1.—The punctuation marks used in fonografic writing are:

× or · .Period—Used at the end of complete sentences.

......Dash—Used in a break of sentences.

..Parenthesis—Used to enclose parenthetical remarks.

Bracket—Used to enclose remarks by reporter or editor.

Hyphen—Used to indicate compound words.

.....Emphasis—Used to indicate emphatic words and sentences.

.........Capitalizer—Used to denote capitalization or name, and the words *equal to*.

........Pleasantry or Laughter—Used to denote mirthful feeling.

.........Interrogation—Used to denote a question.

.........Exclamation—Used to indicate feeling, pathos, wonder or surprise.

All other punctuation marks used in writing and printing must be supplied in the transcripts made of one's shorthand notes.

2.—Capital letters are indicated thus:

E, O, N. Y., Lima.

3.—In letter writing, or in memoranda, the vowel initials of names, if preferred, can be expressed by their signs written in the correct vowel place by side of the cancelled *Te* stem, thus:

E, O.

4.—To indicate emphasis in print, words are set in italic letters. To indicate emphasis in longhand writing, words are underscored by a straight, horizontal line. To indicate emphasis in fonografic writing, words are underscored by a waved line. Illustration

Best *merry*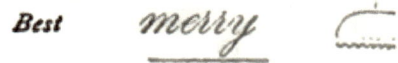

LESSON V.

DIFTHONGS, OR COMPOUND VOWELS.

1.
i	oi	ow	ew
My	b*oy*'s	*ow*l	fl*ew*.

DIFTHONG SIGNS.

˅	˃	˄	˂
i	oi	ow	ew

2. The difthong signs are derived from the letter ✕ , or inclined cross, thus:

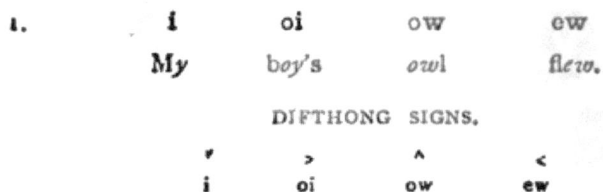

Observe that in writing these signs, the angle should be made sharper than is shown in the cross.

3. The difthong signs possess fixed values, and are written in the most convenient place,—usually the *third* place.

4. The difthong following *r*, as in *rude, rumor, rule*, etc., is not so sharp as that heard in *pure, cure, beauty*, etc., but the same sign is used to represent both.

5. Initial difthongs should be written first, and, if convenient, joined to the following stem. Illustration: ↱. *Ida,* ↰ *ivy,* ↱ *ice.*

6.—READING EXERCISE

ON DIFTHONGS.

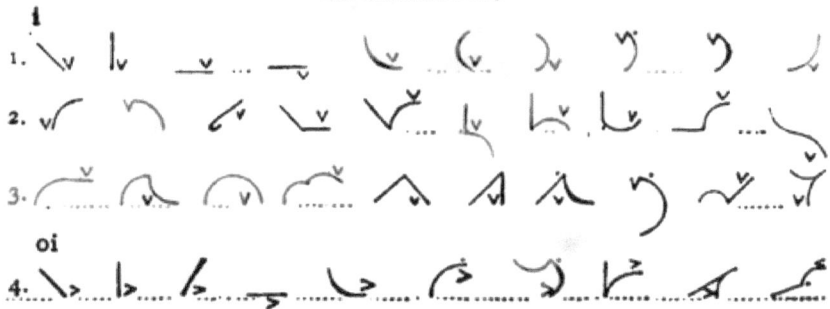

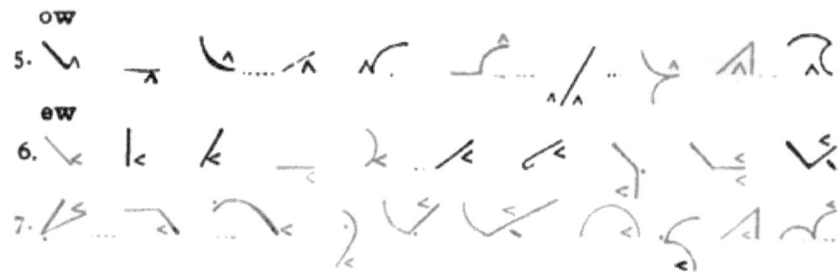

7.—WRITING EXERCISE
ON DIFTHONGS.

Pie, tie, Ida, Ike, Guy, fie, vie, **ivy,** thigh, sigh, ice, eyes, **shy,** lie, lye, **ally,** nigh, high, **isle,** aisle, **pipe,** pike, pile, abide, byway, tidy, tithe, time, tiny, dike, dime, idol, chime, **China,** jibe, kite, chyle, chyme, guide, guile, Fido, five, shiny, like, **life,** alive, lime, imbibe, mighty, mile, knife, hypo, height, hide.

Boy, boil, **toy,** toil, joy, coy, coil, Voy, avoid, **alloy,** oil, annoy, **noisy,** ahoy.

Bow, Dow, **cow,** vow, **row, owl,** owlish (*ow-La-Sha*), chow-chow, couch, gouge, fowl, foul, **avowed,** vouch, loud, mouth.

Pew, dew, adieu, due, **chew, Jew, cue,** thew, Sue, lieu, hew, hue, Hugh, huge, beauty, duty, **dupe, duke,** eschew, juror, juicy, July, Jehu, cube, imbue, mule.

Write *Er* **for** *r* in the following words: **Ire,** pyre, attire, dire, gyre (*Ja-Er*), fire, lyre, tire, Irish (*i-Er-Ish*), toiler, **lure, allure** (*El-Er*).

Write *Ra* **for** *r* in the following words: Rye, wry, ripe, right, rite, write, Wright, arrive, writhe, **irate,** aright, mire, roy, roil (*Ra-El*), roilly (*Ra-La*), rout, rowdy, rue, pursue, bureau, jury, fury, furore, rude, review.

Write *El* for *l* in the following words: File, **Nile,** foil, roil. Hoyle, fowl, foul.

LESSON VI.

JOINED VOWEL-TICKS.

1. A vowel (belonging either to the *dot* or *dash* class), following a difthong, is more quickly and conveniently represented by a small tick joined to the difthong sign, and written in the direction of *Te* on *oi* and *ew*, and of *Ka* on *i* and *ow*.

2.—READING EXERCISE
ON JOINED VOWEL TICKS.

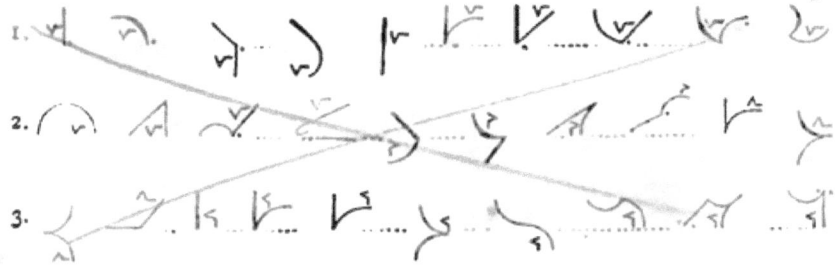

3.—WRITING EXERCISE
ON JOINED VOWEL TICKS.

Iota, Iowa, Iona, piety, pious, bias, Tioga, diet, dial, Viola, scion, Zion, boyish, coyish, voyage, towel, dewy, Dewey, Jewess, duel, dual, jewel, jewish, Shuey, annuity.

Write *Er* for *r* in the following words: Dyer, power, tower, dower, shower, jeweler, fewer, sewer, newer.

Write *Ra* for *r* in the following words: Diary, fiery, riot, Ryan, miry, higher, royal (*Ra-El*) royally (*Ra-La*), cower, Rowell (*Ra-El*), jewelry, ruin, renewal (*El* stem), hewer.

Write *El* for *l* in the following words: Vial, viol, lion, royal, vowel, Rowell, Howell, fuel, Newell, renewal.

CIRCLES AND LOOPS.

LESSON VII.

BRIEF ADDITIONAL SIGNS FOR S AND Z.

1. The frequently occurring sounds of *s* and *z* are, in a large class of words, represented by a small circle, ○, named *Ĭs* or *Ĭz*, used at the beginning of stems, between stems, and at the end of stems, thus securing convenience in joining, brevity of outline, and greater ease and rapidity in writing.

2. The circle is joined to straight stems by a *leftward* motion of the pen, moving in three distinct directions, as shown in this little square joined initially to the *Pe* stem, ↙, while a fourth direction forms the stem.

3. The circle is always written on the concave side of a curve thus:

4. In joining the circle to *any* stem, either initially or finally, let the *first* and *last* movements be at *right angles* with the stem. Illustration:

Let the learner practise on the squares until without their aid a perfect circle can be easily formed.

5. The circle has no effect upon vowelization. A vowel heard either *before* or *after* a consonant represented by a *stem* is always written *before* or *after* the stem, whether a circle is on the stem or not. Illustration: *up*, *sup*, *pie*, *spy*, *eat*, *seat*, *ache*, *sake*.

6. A vowel is *never* read *before* an initial circle. The initial circle *always* reads *first*, and then any vowel that may be *before* the stem, and then the *stem*, and then any vowel that may *follow* the stem. Illustration: *settee*, *satiety*, *soda*. See page 24, line 4.

7. Initial *s* is expressed on the *Hah* stem by a circle in the place of the hook. Illustration: ⚞ *Soho*. See line 4, seventh and eighth words of page 24.

8. Initial *s* is always represented by the stem. See page 25, line 16.

9. The circle at the end of stems is always read last. A vowel cannot read *after* a circle because the circle furnishes no *places* in which three different vowels could be written. See page 24, line 5.

10. A circle between two straight stems running in the *same* direction, is written by the same motion of the pen as the circle on a single straight stem. See page 24, line 6.

11. A circle between straight stems, struck in different directions, is written *outside* of the angle. See page 24, line 7.

12. A circle between a straight line and a curve, is always written on the concave side of the curve. See page 25, line 8.

13. A circle between *Em* and any other curve, when it cannot come within the curve of *both* stems, is written on the concave side of *Em*. See page 25, line 9.

14. A circle between *Ef*, *Un*, and *La*, and between *La* and *Ve*, and *La* and *Ith*, is written on the concave side of *La*. See page 25, line 10.

15. The circle between other curve combinations is written on the concave side of both curves. See page 25, line 11.

LARGE CIRCLE FOR SES, SEZ, ZEZ.

16. The double sound of *s* or *z*—*ses, sez, zez*—is expressed by a *large* circle in such words as—

passes, possess, teases, possessed, excessive, races.

17. The use of a double-sized circle to express the double sound of *s* and *z*, allows the plural ending of words to be formed in analogy with words in the singular number terminating with the small circle. Illustration:

piece, pieces, case, cases, rose, roses;

also the third person singular of such verbs as end with the small circle is expressed with the large circle. Illustration:

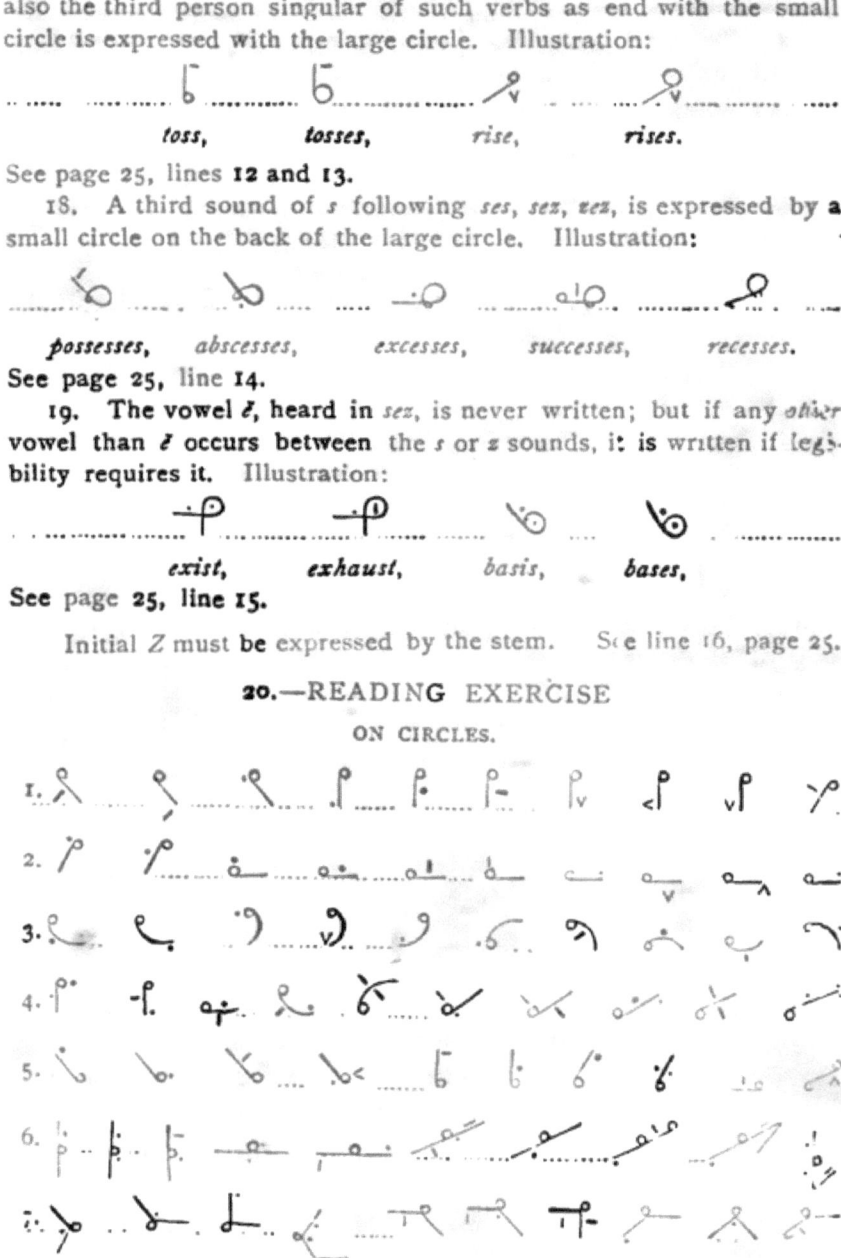

toss, *tosses,* *rise,* *rises.*

See page 25, lines **12** and **13**.

18. A third sound of *s* following *ses, sez, zez,* is expressed by a small circle on the back of the large circle. Illustration:

possesses, *abscesses,* *excesses,* *successes,* *recesses.*

See page 25, line **14**.

19. The vowel *ĕ*, heard in *sez*, is never written; but if any other vowel than *ĕ* occurs between the *s* or *z* sounds, it is written if legibility requires it. Illustration:

exist, *exhaust,* *basis,* *bases,*

See page 25, line **15**.

Initial *Z* must be expressed by the stem. See line 16, page 25.

20.—READING EXERCISE
ON CIRCLES.

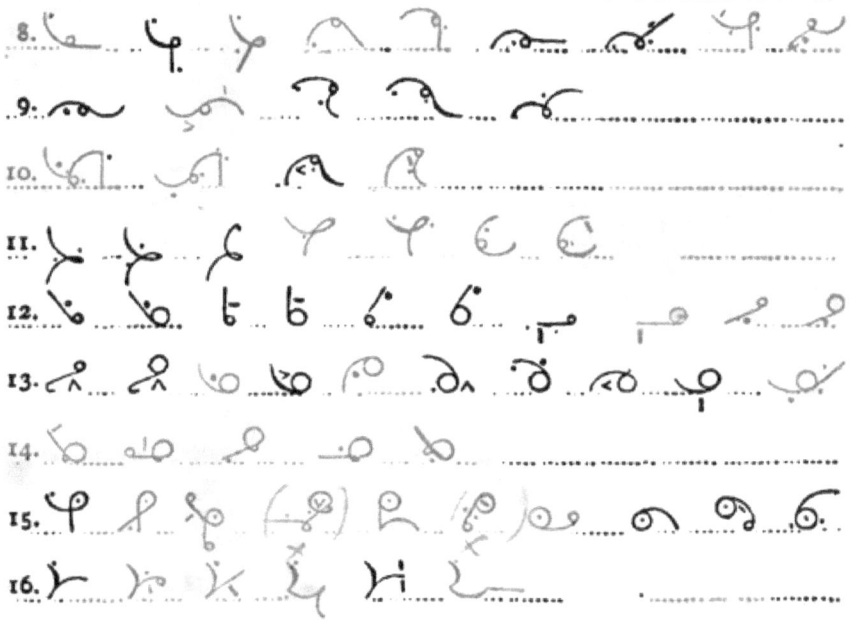

21.—WRITING EXERCISE
ON CIRCLES.

Soap, **soup, sips, saps,** seat, stays, stows, stew, suit, sight, sty, seed, said, **sad, sawed,** sowed, soda, suds, **seeds,** sage, sages, seige, sedge, sausages, **seek, sake, sick,** sacks, success, successes, Sussex, sag, sago, safe, sofa, **save,** seive, sythe, **size, sizes, scize,** seizes, sash, sashes, seal, seals, sails, sale, solo, **sorry,** sorrows, sore, sere, **sour,** sire, sir, **Sam,** seam, sum, psalm, **sin,** son, sun, sane, **sign, sneeze,** snows, sing, sang, sung, sway, sways, **S**wiss, Soho, Sahara.

Pass, piece, **peace, passes, pieces,** pace, paces, pause, pauses, posses, possesses, base, bays, **boys,** abase, abases, abuse, abscess, abscesses, tease, teases, days, dose, doze, dozes, disease, diseases, cheese, cheeses, chase, chews, etches, ages, **joys,** Jews, juice, rejoice, rejoices, kiss, kisses, Cass, Cass's, case, **cases,** oaks, aches, echoes, ox, **ax,** axes, axis, axes, excess, excesses, excuse, excuses, exercise, exercises, **exercised,** guess, guesses, gaze, geese, goose, gas, gases, gauze, Guy's, **face,** faces, vase, vases, vice, vices, voice, voices vows, views, reviews, thighs, oaths, shows, shoes, **ashes**, lace, laces, loose, looses, lose, loses, lease, allays, alleys, Ellis, Alice, raise, (*Ra* for *r*) raises, **race, races,** recess, recesses, rise; arise, (*Er* for *r*) arises, arouse, arouses, erase, erases, **ears,** oars, **errs, airs,** miss, misses, muss, aims, noise, annoys, **noises,** nose, niece, nice, ounce, ounces, woes, woos, yeas, hose, haze, **hiss,** hisses, **house,** houses, **hews, hues,** Hughes, hies, Hayes, pushes, bushes, tushes (upward stem, *Sha*, for *sh* following *Te, De, Ef, La, Ra,* and *Hah*), dishes, **dashes,** fishes, **lashes,** luscious, **rushes,** hushes, possessed, pacify, passive, passeth, **pestle** (*p-s-l*), **puzzle, poison,** obesity, beset, besides, beseech, basks, **abusive,** bustle (*b-s-l*), **baser,** besom, business, basin, baseness, **ab**sence, upset, tasty, outside, **task,** tassel, **teasel,** desk, dusk, dusky, dusty, decides, decisive, diseased, docile (**either upward** or downward *l*), desire, desirous, disrobe, dislike, dispels, disloyal, dozen, Chesapeake, **chosen, chisel,** Jason, jostle, cusp, cask, **cassock,** excessive, chasm, cosmos, **cousin,** Casino, castle (*k-s-l*), Castile (*k-s-t-l*), gasp, gossip, gusto, **guzzle,** fiasco, fizzle (*El* stem), fossil, **vessel,** vassal, visage, thistle (*El* stem), lisp, receive (*r-s-v*), misty, mask, listen (*El* stem), lessen, lesson, loosen, reason, **risen,** rosin, resume remiss, missile, muzzle, music, musk, mosque, **mistletoe** (*m-z-l*), mouser (*Ra* stem), miser, misery, honesty, nasty, **necessity,** necessary, nestle, nozzle, **insist,** resist, subsist, desist, **system, scissors,** saucer, season, Susan, **schism,** Sicily, successive, **unsafe,** unseen, Owasco, anxiety, anxious (*Ing-Ish-Is*), **hasty,** hastily, **husk,** hassock, **husky,** hustle (*La* stem), hasten, Hosannah, **hussar** (*Ra* stem)

SHORT SENTENCES.

Miss Dewey's **roses.** Laura's peaches. Olive's mosses. **Leave** Johnny's books. Naughty Darius Howe **chews** gum. **Katie** loves nice, rich coffee. Miss Lillie **Snow** ate savory soup. Choose right ways. Resist laziness. Lizzie eats ripe, juicy pears. **Maurice's** slow coach. Sadie's ice houses. Newell Dyer's sons rise early. Viola passes Jennie's house. Sadie supposes wrongs. Lucy loves Johnny. Susan rose sad. Lizzie sings Katie's merry song. Johnny's cows eat **husks.** Dogs **chase** cows. Mollie hates snow. Chicago's chime-bells ring merry music. Tommy's owl eats mice. Honesty satisfies **reason.** Boys leap slow. Lena loves rainy **days. Seek** happiness.

LESSON VIII.

LOOPS FOR *ST* AND *STR*.

1. A small loop written initially on stems expresses *initial st* sounds; written finally, expresses *final st* or *zd* sounds. Illustration: *step*, *state*, *steak*, *still*, *star*, *starry*, *stem*, *stony*, *past* or *passed*, *guest* or *guessed*, *mist* or *missed*, *honest*, *abused*, *gazed*, *aroused*, *housed*. See lines 1–3 below.

2. A large final loop on stems expresses *str*. Illustration: *pastor*, *toaster*, *faster*, *Lester*, *yester*. See line 4 below.

3. A circle is written on the back of loops to express *s* or *z* following *st* or *str*. Illustration: *posts*, *posters*. See line 5 below.

4. The loops can be used in the *middle* of words provided, at the point of junction, the stems do not cross each other. If the stems cross, the loop is reduced to the value of the *s* circle. Illustration: *destiny*, *testify*, *yesterday*. See line 6 below.

5.—READING EXERCISE
ON ST AND STR LOOP.

6.—WRITING EXERCISE
ON ST AND STR LOOPS.

Steep, step, stop, stoop, stab, stub, state, **stout,** steady, study, stitch, stage, steak, stake, stick, stack, stalk, stock, stuck, stucco, stag, stiff, stuff, staff, stave, stove, Stacy, steal, steel, stale, stall stole, stool, still, stilly, Stella, **style, steer,** star, store, starry, **story, steam, stem,** stony, sting, stung.

Pieced, paste, paced, pest, pester, past, passed, posts, **posters,** beasts, **baste, boasts,** boaster, boost, bust, busts, abased, abused, teased, **taste, toast, toaster, tests,** attest, dost, dust, dusters, adduced, **doused,** chaste, **chased, chests, Chester's,** jests, joist, cased, kissed, last, castor, coast, coaster, costs, Custer's, gazed, guests, guessed, ghosts, aghast, feasts, faced, **fist,** fast, faster, fussed, Foster, vest, vast, vaster, least, laced, list, lest, Lester's, last, luster, loosed, erased, erst, arrest, aroused, raced, roast, roaster, wrist, rust, roused, roosts, roosters, mists, missed, asts, masters, amassed, amused, most, musters, nests, Nast, honest, Nestor, songster, songsters, waste, **waists,** West, Wistar, Worcester (Wooster), **yeast,** yester.

Artist (*Ra* for *r*), artists, reduced, richest, rejoiced, refused, **revised,** upraised, ballast, **tallest,** utmost, teamster, dullest, coolest, calmest, mildest, **forests, forester, fensed,** evinced, announced,

7.—SHORT SENTENCES.

Lester likes rest. Teamster Post chased Chester West. Wistar's stomache stuff. Worcester's best yeast. Coolest, dullest, tallest forester. Songsters sing artistic music, announced. Stella's music kissed **starry** luster in stilly **eve.** Jack's master testifies last. Costly stove **paste.** Jesters master songsters. Teamsters waste costly dusters. Artistic songsters master **music.** Hester testifies lest ministers sophistry master reason.

SEMICIRCLES AND HOOK.

LESSON IX.

BRIEF SIGNS FOR *WA* AND *YA*.

SEMICIRCLES.

Wĕ, Wŭ, Yĕ, Yŭ.

1. Small semicircles for *w* and *y* are employed in a large class of words, adding greatly to legibility, and facilitating ease and speed of writing. Illustration:

weep, web, waits, watch, walks, yacht, yokes, unyoke, yellow.

2. The small circle is conveniently written within *Wĕ* and *Wŭ* signs to express *sw* in certain words. Illustration:

sweep, sweet, swig, swings, suavity.

WA HOOK ON LA, RA, EM, UN.

3. Brief *Wa* is joined to *La, Ra, Em,* and *Un,* as a hook. Illustration: *wail, wore, wem, wen.* See next page, lines 6-7.

4. The circle for initial *s* is written on the *Wa* hook of *Ra*, but never on the hooks of *La, Em,* and *Un*—the circle and *Wa* stem being used for *sw* preceding these three stems. Illustration: *swore, swells.* See next page, line 8.

YI, YOI, YOW.

5. The trifthongs *yi, yoi, yow,* are expressed by brief *Ya* joined to the difthong signs. Illustration:

genii, Honeoye, meow.

NOTE (*a*).—In joining *Wŭ* to *Pe, Be, Ka, Ga,* and *Ing,* observe that the motions of the pen are similar to those made in forming a plain figure 2.

(*b*).—In joining *Wĕ* to *Te, De, Cha, Ja,* and *Ish,* observe that the motions of the pen are like those made in forming a figure 9, while *Yĕ* is joined to *Te, De,* and *Ith,* by a motion similar to that in forming a figure 7.

6.—READING EXERCISE
ON BRIEF WA AND YA SIGNS.

7.—WRITING EXERCISE
ON BRIEF WA AND YA SIGNS.

Wipe, web, Webster, witty, wittily, wet, wettest, **wait**, witticism, weeds, wade, wades, widows, widest, witch, bewitch, watch, wage, wedge, weak, **wake**, walk, woke, wicks, **wax, waxes**, waxed, **wigs**, wife, waif, woof, weave, weaves, wives, withe, wash, wing, **wings**.

Sweep, swop, **swoop**, swab, **sweet, sweeter**, sweetest, sweetly, **sweat**, Swede, swayed, **switch**, swig, suave, suavity, swath, swathe, **swash**, swing, swung, **assuage**, assuages, unswayed, unswathe, Zouave.

Weal, **wail**, wall, wallow, **wool**, wooly, Wallace, Willis, Wells, willow, welcome, wellfare, wealth, unwell, unwieldy, unwelcome, wealthy, Willoughby, war, wore, weary, wary, worry, wear, ware, wares, beware, worse, worst, worth, worthless, worthy, unworthy, warm, worm, wormwood, swore, swear, swears, soirée, swarm, swarms, swarthy, wammel, wem, wean, wane, win, wins, winnow, wen, wan, won, wanes, wince, winces, winced, windy, window.

queen, queenly, **quince,** quinces, equinox, **twine, twines, entwine,** twin, **twins,** twain, **twinge,** twinges, piquancy, twirl, queer, qualm, wigwam, quincy, quench, **quinzy,** quantum, Dwinnell, quano, query, quarry, **Edwin.**

Yacht, yoke, unyoke, **yak,** youth, Uriah, Yulee, Yale, yell, yellow, yellowish, (upward stem for *sh*), yawl, yelp, yelk, yore, (*Er* stem), yarrow, (*Ra* stem), **yam,** yon, yawns, Eunice, uinique, unity, young, youngster, yank.

Genii, Honeoye, meow.

8.—SHORT SENTENCES.

Willie Wallace works. Willie Woods sings sweetly. Eunice waxes warm. Young Yulee's yacht. Worthy's young wife. Winnie's weak kitty " meows " Wednesday. Yellow dogs wag yellow tails. Wet dogs yelp. Willis sweeps. Edwin's wife walks Wednesday. Wage war young swells, unworthy youths. Willie's bees swarm warm windy wet days. Swing young wives sweetly. Dissuade Webster's unwelcome youngster. Welcome wealth, worthy youths.

LESSON X.

BRIEF *WA* AND *YA* SIGNS DISJOINED.

1. The semicircles for the coalescents, *W*(*oo*) *Y*(*é*) cannot be conveniently joined **between** stems **or** at the end of stems, in a large class of words—especially words containing the *y*(*é*) element—and are, therefore, disjoined and **written in** the vowel places, taking the order of **vowel** sounds and made *heavy* when in the place of *long* vowels and *light* when in the place of *short* ones.

2. Tabular view **of brief** *Wa* and *Ya* in vowel places:

WA SERIES.

	Long.				Short.	
⊂ **wē**	in	week	⊂ wĭ	**in**	wit
⊂ **wā**	"	wake	⊂ wĕ	"	wet
⊂ **wā**	"	waft	⊂ wă	"	wag
⊃ wā	in	wall	⊃ wō	in	wot
⊃ wō	"	woke	⊃ wu	"	wun
⊃ woo	"	wooed	⊃ woo	"	wool

YA SERIES.

	Long.				Short.	
ᴗ **yē**	in	year	ᴗ **yĭ**	**in**	**yit**
ᴗ ya	"	yale	ᴗ yĕ	"	yet
ᴗ ya	"	yard	ᴗ yă	"	yak
ᴖ ya	in	yawn	ᴖ yo	in	yon
ᴖ yo	"	yoke	ᴖ yu	"	young
ᴖ yoo	"	you	ᴖ yoo	"	Yucatan

NOTE (*a*).—The *w* signs are made from a circle cut in **two** vertically, thus: ⊖ while for the *y* signs it is cut in **two** horizontally, thus: ⊖

(*b*).—The **w sign in** dot vowel **places opens to** the *right*, or towards the *east*, while **the *w* sign in dash vowel places** opens **to the** *left* **or towards the** *west;* and the *y* sign in dot vowel places opens *upward*, or towards the *north*, while the *y* sign in dash vowel places, opens *downward*, or towards the *south*.

NOTE (*c*).—Observe that the vowel sound in *Wĭ* and *Yĭ* is that of a *dot vowel*, hence *Wĭ* and *Yĭ* are the signs used in the *dot-vowel* places.

(*d*).—The vowel sound in *Wŭ* and *Yŭ* is that of a *dash vowel*, hence *Wŭ* and *Yŭ* are used in *dash-vowel* places.

W AND Y EQUIVALENTS.

3. Before giving a list of words illustrating the use of the disjoined semicircles, it will be an advantage to the student to understand clearly the alfabetic equivalents of *w* and *y*.

The sound represented by *w* is the same as *u* in *quick* and nearly the same as *oo* in *coo* (being briefer in pronunciation than *oo*, and in some words more like *oo* in *foot*), and the final element of the difthongs *o, ow, ew,*—as will be easily perceived by the slow pronunciation of *o—o-oo, ow—ah-oo, ew—e-oo*.

4. The sounds represented by *y* in *you* and *pity* are the same as *e* in *be* and *i* in *it;* but, when followed by another vowel sound in such words as beaut*eo*us, *opi*ate, etc., the *e* becomes shorter and the *i* sharper, producing a short sound like unaccented *e* in the syllable *be* in behold. *Y-a, e-a,* and *i-a; y-o, e-o,* and *i-o*, when quickly pronounced, are one and the same thing. For example, the syllable *io* in *folio*, can be spelt three ways—*folio, folio, folyo*—and indicate the same pronunciation.

5. The following words contain *w(oo)* and *y(ē)* sounds represented in different ways by alfabetic equivalents, without changing the pronunciation: Iowa—Io-ooa—Ioa; Owen—Oooen—Oen; bowie—bo-ooy—bo-I; boa—bo-ooa—bowa; bivouac—bivooac—bivwac, quick—kooik—kwik; twig—tooig—tuig; sweet—sooeet—sueet; Yale—ēale—Iāle—; yank—ēank—Iänk; India—Indea—Indya; opiate—opeāte—opyate; atheist—athI-Ist—athyist; carrier—carre-er—carryer; anterior—antereor—antery-or.

6. There are a few words in which the syllabication might seem changed by the use of a sign that suggested the letter *y*—such as ⌣ *barrier*, ⌣ *merrier*, the fonografic forms of which suggest the spelling of the words with a *y* and *two r's*, instead of *three*, thus: *meryer, baryer*, and syllabized thus, *mer-yer, bar-yer*, instead of thus, *mery-er, bary-er;* but as there are no such words as *mer-yer* and *bar-yer*, no confusion can arise by the use of the *y* sign. The words *collier (yer), lawyer*, etc., would never be pronounced *colly-er, lawy-er*, for the reason that there are no such words in the language. English speaking students will have no difficulty in distinguishing between these two classes of words.

7. There are a few concurrent vowels—the initial one of which is accented—which better be expressed by their separate signs, thus:

idea,   *plan,*   *séance,*   *éon,*   *éolis,*   *Léo,*   *Léon,*

writing nearest to the stem that vowel which is heard *next* to the stem.

8. The concurrent vowels in such words as *bowie, boa, doughy, Owen,* etc., are more conveniently and quickly expressed by the dash for *o* and a brief *w* sign joined, than by the exact vowel signs written separately—taking advantage of the terminal *oo* or *w* element of *o*, and representing it by the brief *w* sign, which sign carries with it, or, at least, suggests on account of its names, *Wĕ* and *Wŭ*, an accompanying short vowel sound, dot or dash, according to the direction in which it opens. Illustration: bowie, doughy, or Owen, oasis — using *Wĕ,* because it represents *w* with a dot vowel sound following it. boa, Noah — using *Wŭ,* because it represents *w* with a dash vowel sound following it — the vowel sounds in these words being invariably pronounced in ordinary speech (even by the best scholars), nearer like the vowel in *up* than like short *ah.* By taking advantage of this pronunciation a distinction can be made between boa, and bowie Noe and Noah, etc., etc.

NOTE.—While it may seem teaching a tautophonical pronunciation to represent the vanish or terminal sound of *o* by both the *o* dash and brief *w* sign attached to the *o* dash, it is necessary to so represent it in order to secure a sign that will *join* legibly to the dash and at the same time represent, or suggest, the short vowel sound following the *o* sound. The student may regard that the dash represents the radical or initial sound of *o* (short, as in *whole*), while the *w* sign represents *both* the vanish or terminal sound of *o* and the short vowel following it; or he may, if preferred, regard the dash as representing full *o*, and brief *w* sign as representing only the short vowel following. Either way, it expresses the same thing.

OF PHONOGRAPHY. 35

9. The concurrent vowels of *poet, poem, bowie, boa, towage, Zoe, Noe,* if expressed by their separate signs, are written thus:

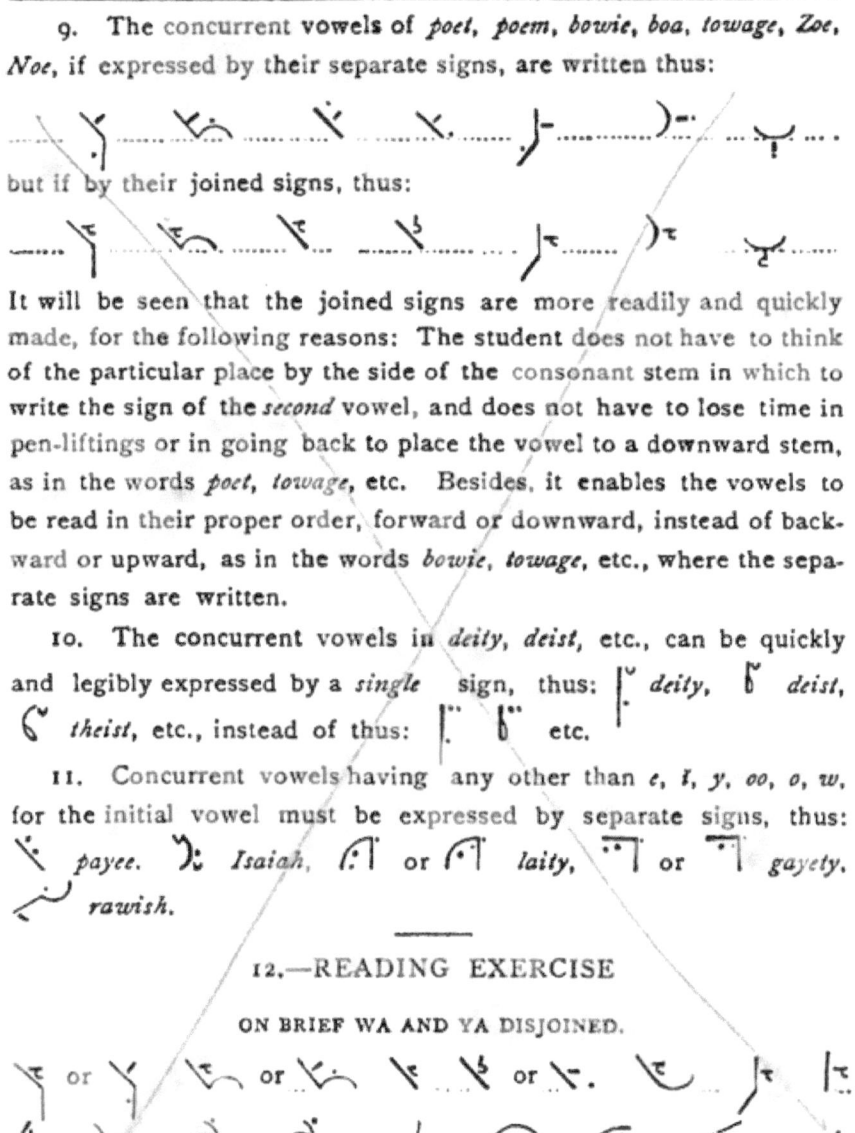

but if by their joined signs, thus:

It will be seen that the joined signs are more readily and quickly made, for the following reasons: The student does not have to think of the particular place by the side of the consonant stem in which to write the sign of the *second* vowel, and does not have to lose time in pen-liftings or in going back to place the vowel to a downward stem, as in the words *poet, towage,* etc. Besides, it enables the vowels to be read in their proper order, forward or downward, instead of backward or upward, as in the words *bowie, towage,* etc., where the separate signs are written.

10. The concurrent vowels in *deity, deist,* etc., can be quickly and legibly expressed by a *single* sign, thus: *deity, deist, theist,* etc., instead of thus: etc.

11. Concurrent vowels having any other than *e, i, y, oo, o, w,* for the initial vowel must be expressed by separate signs, thus: *payee, Isaiah,* or *laity,* or *gayety, rawish.*

12.—READING EXERCISE

ON BRIEF WA AND YA DISJOINED.

or   or   or   .

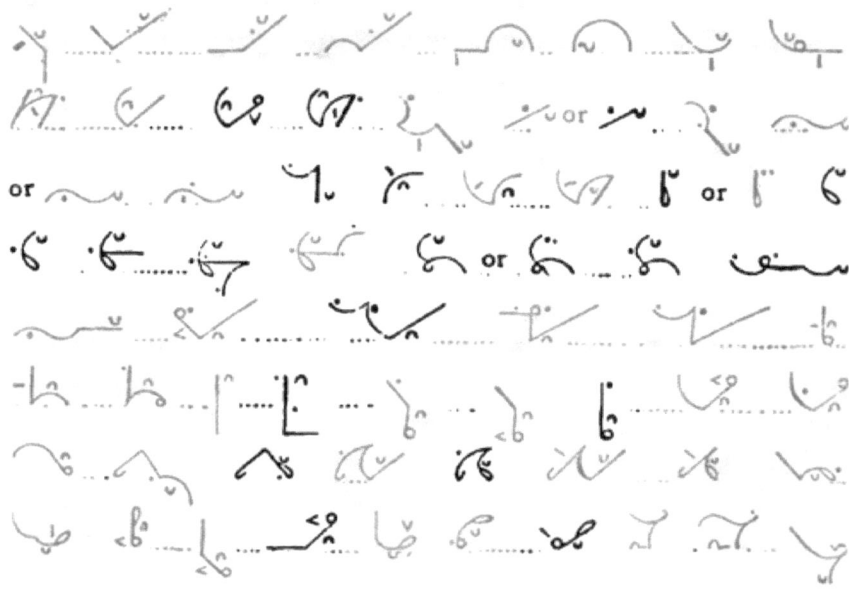

13.—WRITING EXERCISE

ON BRIEF WA AND YA DISJOINED.

Poets, poetic, poem, bowie-knife, boa, towage, doughy, **Zoe**, showy, Louis (Looi), lower, Louisa, rower, mower, Noe, **Noel**, Noah, hoer, oasis, oases, stoic, Stowell, snowy, slowest, soloist.

Opiate, barrier, carrier, **merrier**, Collier, lawyer, piano, **fiasco**, geology, **theology, theory, theories,** theorize, theorized, **Zenobia, Zenia, area, Arabia, mania, ammonia, India, olio,** folio, folios, **foliage, deist, deistic,** theist, atheist, **atheistic,** atheistical, atheistically, **atheism,** insignia, maniac, superior, exterior, inferior, interior, anterior, **odious,** odium, idiom, idiot, idiocy, idiotic, piteous, beauteous, tedious, copious, copiously, furious, various, impious, happier, happiest, wealthier, wealthiest, worthier, worthiest, balmiest, funniest, studious, studiously, dubious, curious, **tinier, tiniest,** sorriest, silliest, **annual, manual,** biennial.

Payee, pean, idea, gayety, séance, Isaiah, **laity, Leo, Leon,** eolis, rawish, eon.

ASPIRATE TICK, HEH.
LESSON XI.
HEH ON STEMS.

1. A small inclined tick for initial *h*, is used on the following stems: *Em*, *Er*, and *Wa*. Illustration:

home, homely, harm, whistle.

2. *Heh* is also used on the joined brief *w* signs and hook, made in the direction of *Pe* or *Cha*, and written upward or downward according to convenience of joining. Ilustration:

whip, wheat, whack, whiff, whale, whir, whine, whim.

3.—READING EXERCISE
ON ASPIRATE TICK.

4.—WRITING EXERCISE
ON ASPIRATE TICK.

Hymn, hem, ham, hum, hemal, Hummel, homely, homeliness, homeless, homelike, homicide, homo, homily, hominy, humility, hammock, harm, harmless, harmony, harmonize.

Whey, whoa, whiz, whizzes, whist, whisker, whizzed, whistle, whistler, whisk, whiskey, whiskers.

Whip, Whipple, whop, whopper, wheat, Whateley, Whitelaw, whittle, Whitcher, whack, whacks, whig, whiff, whang.

Whale, whaler, Wheeling, whir, whirs, whirl, whirligig, wharl, wherry, wharf, wharves, whim, whimsical, whine.

ABBREVIATIONS AND POSITION.

LESSON XII.

ABBREVIATIONS.

1. There are certain words of common, frequent use, that, for the sake of greater speed in writing, are abbreviated in their fonografic representation, the same as words are abbreviated in common print; that is, expressed by one, two, or more of their letters or **signs**, instead of all. About two-thirds of these abbreviations **are** complete in their *consonant* representation—the *vowels* only being omitted; and although the advanced fonografer never writes the vowels in any word, except when absolutely necessary, these *special* words—with vowels, only, omitted—are placed in the list of abbreviations, because they are *never* to be vowelized but learned as the special, fixed signs for those words; while the words not in the list of abbreviations are vowelized or not, as the writer finds necessary.

2. Some words are abbreviated by omitting the **consonants, retaining** only the vowel, while other words, still, **are** represented by **brief signs** such as the circle, loops, half-circles, etc.

VOWEL RULE OF POSITION.

3. Before giving a list of abbreviations it will **be** necessary **to** explain what is termed "The vowel rule of position." It is already well understood that there are *three* PLACES by the side **of** a consonant stem for vowels. Corresponding to these three *vowel* PLACES are three *stem* or *outline* POSITIONS governed by the vowels: Words containing a *first place* **vowel to** be written in *first position—above* the line; words containing a *second place* **vowel to** be written in *second position—on* the line; words containing a *third place* vowel **to** be **written** in *third position—thru* or *under* the line.

4. The *first* position for *upright* and *inclined* stems is HALF the height of a *Te* stem above the line; and for horizontals and brief signs, about HALF-WAY BETWEEN the lines of writing, according to the width between the lines—writing a little below the centre on widened paper.

5. The *second* position for *all* signs is **on the** line of writing.

6. The *third* position for *upright* and *inclined* stems is THROUGH or ACROSS, the line; and for horizontals and brief signs, UNDER the line.

7. It is a great **aid to** legibility to write, **not only** the greater number of abbreviations, but also words of ONE SYLLABLE in the *position* indicated by the vowel—or accented vowel, if a word contain **more than** one.

8. Some of the abbreviations are not written **according to the** "**vowel** rule of position."

(*a*).—This occurs **where** there are two or more words having the **same** outline and containing **vowels** of the same class; they require to be written in different positions to prevent conflict and confusion, as well as hesitancy in reading. See signs for *do* and *had, each* and *which, if* and *for,* etc.

(*b*).—Again, where **there is but *one* word of a certain** stem or outline, it is always written in second position, regardless of the vowel rule, because that position is the **most natural, and favors ease and speed of writing.** See sign for *your.*

(*c*).—Where there are two words **of the same** outline **and vowel** class, the most frequently-occurring one is given the second position. See signs for *each* and *which, ease* and *was, **law** and will, are* and *our, no* and *own.*

(*d*).—Where there are two words of the same **outline, but differing** vowels, the most frequently occurring one takes the second **position,** regardless of the vowel, and the other one **the next** position **to it.** See *which* and *much, think* and *thank.*

9.—SIMPLE STEMS.—NO. 1.

ARRANGED ACCORDING TO THE FONOGRAFIC ALFABET.

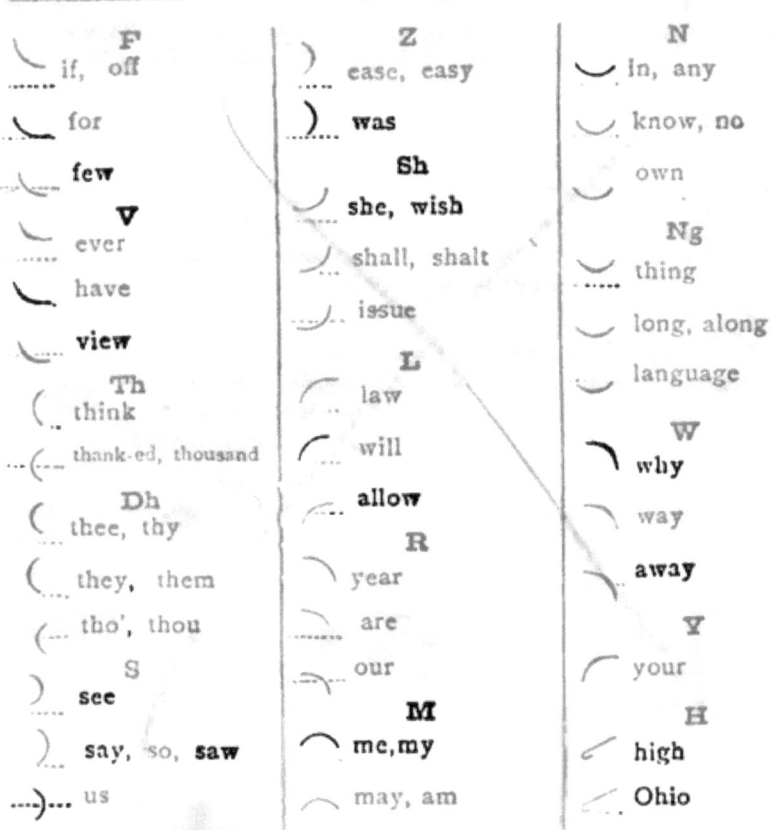

10. Final *s* is added to **any of** the above **signs** by writing the circle **on** the end of the stem.

II.—SHORT SENTENCES.

Pay up your bills. **It will be your** dollar each time they go. It was in my wish. Which **way** will they go? Why do they **ask** them for it? **It was years** ago. They know why it was so **Do** they ever go up? Have they ever thanked? They say so. It will be easy for us. Shall they go away? **They** will wish them much joy. Each company will be large. Do they see any advantage in it? It was to be so. **They may** think so. If they do, she shall know it. Does she own **it?** **No,** she knows it. They had it out each day. Your things are in Ohio.

12.—COMPOUND STEMS.—No. 2.

peculiar-ly-ity	familiar-ly-ity
publish-ed	especially
belong	like
become	look
to become	alike
talk	lawyer
take	irregular-ly-ity
took	argue
dignity	refer
acknowledge	regular-ly-ity
catholic	represent
kill	make
came, come	many, money
effect	among
affect	into
fact	unto
forever	notwithstanding
follow	enjoy

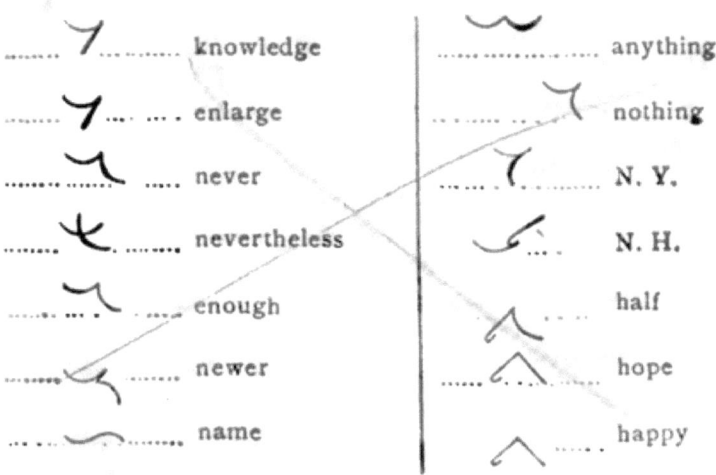

NOTE.—Should the student think these abbreviations difficult to learn, let him notice that very few of them are abbreviated beyond the omission of vowels, so that once looking at them is sufficient to learn them. Those that are abbreviated by the omission of consonants should be written over several times, and then, by practising them in short sentences they will be remembered.

13.—SHORT SENTENCES.

Notwithstanding many peculiar things, they are happy. Nevertheless, anything will do for them Hope for many things. Never follow lawyers. Do nothing half-way. Enjoy knowledge forever. Enlarge your knowledge. Never follow peculiar ways. They came in time for your lawyer's money.

LESSON XIII.

ABBREVIATIONS—Continued.

I.—CIRCLES, LOOPS, AND VOWELS.—NO. 3.

	is, his		themselves
	as, has		says
	first		size
	subject		as well as
	subjected		sir
	best		ours, hours
	its		seem
	said		same, some
	such		something
	just		seen
	suggest		soon
	because		necessary
	signature		most, must
	several		stenographer
	these, thyself		honest
	this		next
	thus, those		wise

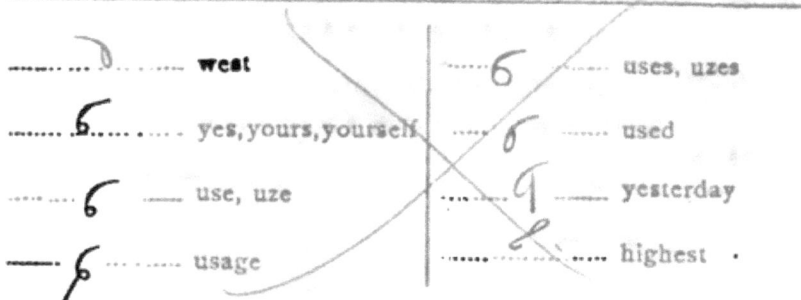

2. The affix "**self**" is expressed **by a** *small* **final circle on stems, and** "selves" by a *large* circle.

3.—WRITING EXERCISE

This is peculiar. **They will** enjoy themselves. This subject was used yesterday. Will they suggest something? She is a first-rate stenographer. Several said **it** was so. Yes, they go West next Wednesday. She is as happy as they are. The boy says his things will come as soon as they wish for them. They have only necessary things. She used yours several times yesterday. They are honest as well as wise. His highest aim is to be just. Be just, because it is best. His signature **is** necessary, as well as yours.

4.—VOWEL SIGNS.—No. 4.

the	two, too	to
a, an	owe, oh, O!	but
and	who-m	should
all	of	I
awe	or	how
ought, aught	on, he, him	6. whose

5.—READING EXERCISE.

6.—WRITING EXERCISE.

The boy has a dog. I see a duck and an owl. They are all up stairs. At sight of it I was in awe. He ought to go soon. Too many of them are in the house. It is too much for him to do. Who took my book? To whom will he go for counsel? He or I must see to it. Will they talk to him? He will go, but I shall stay. Should he think best, they may have it. How soon will he come? Whose book is this? How long have they had it?

LESSON XIV.

ABBREVIATIONS—Continued.

1.—Brief WA and YA Signs.—No. 5.

we	what	yet
with	would	beyond
were	ye	you

2.—Vowel, Stem, and Brief Sign Combinations.—No. 6.

idea		area
now		while
knew, new		well
I'll, I will		where
I'm, I am		aware
already		whereas, worse
altogether		wherever
together		wheresoever
almighty		when
although		one
almost		whence
whoever		once
however		whenever
		whensoever

whencesoever
without
within
withdraw
withal
you're, you are

3.—READING EXERCISE.

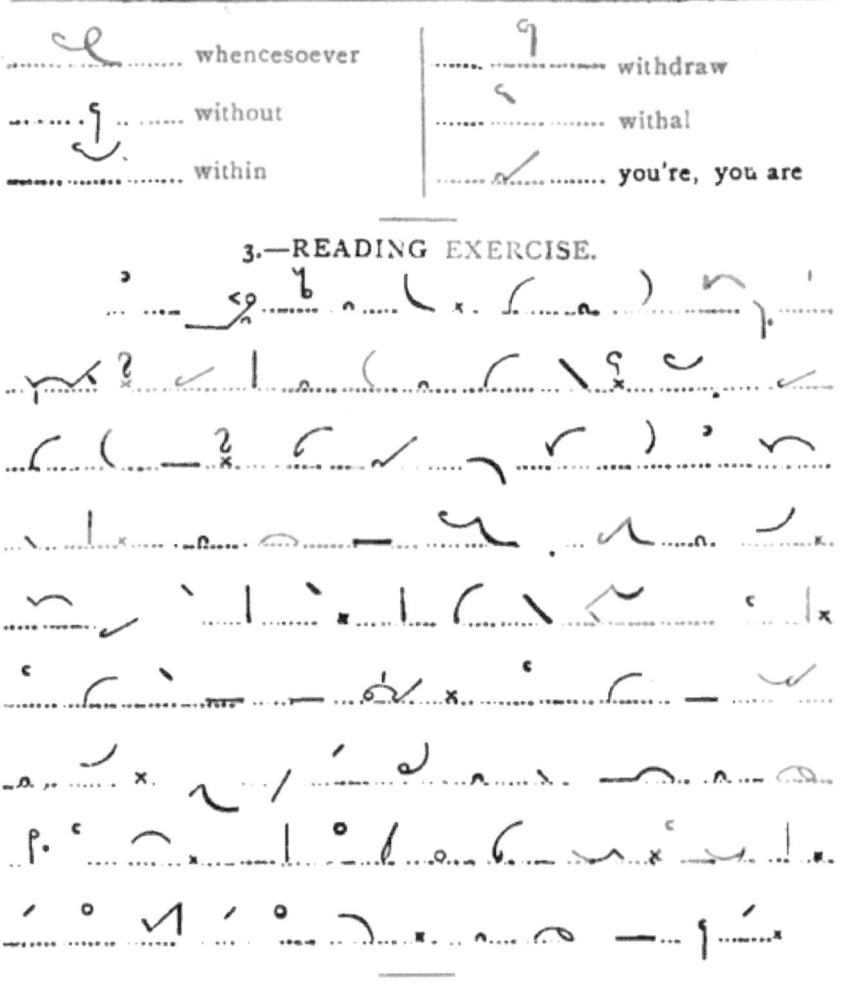

4.—WRITING EXERCISE.

It is **now time** we were on our way. What would **you do for** him? When **and where** would it be best to go? Which **one is it**? What is the area of the **State** in which you live? I hope **she is no** worse. He may go without it altogether. We are within two **miles** of the house. Your ideas will **have weight.** Do **you** know yet how it is? How long ago was it? Whenever **you** are right go **ahead. I am aware** of the fact. Whoever he is we must **see** him.

HALF-LENGTHS AND ED TICK.

LESSON XV.

HALVING STEMS TO ADD *T* OR *D*.

1. A stem can be halved to add the sound of *t* or *d* at the end of words or syllables. Illustration:

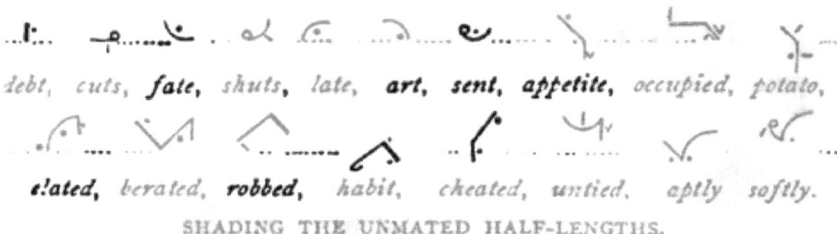

debt, cuts, **fate**, shuts, late, **art**, **sent**, **appetite**, occupied, potato, elated, berated, **robbed**, habit, cheated, untied, aptly softly.

SHADING THE UNMATED HALF-LENGTHS.

2. When the stems *La*, *Er*, *Em*, and *Un*, **are** halved to add *d* let them be shaded; but when halved **to add** *t* let them remain light. Illustration:

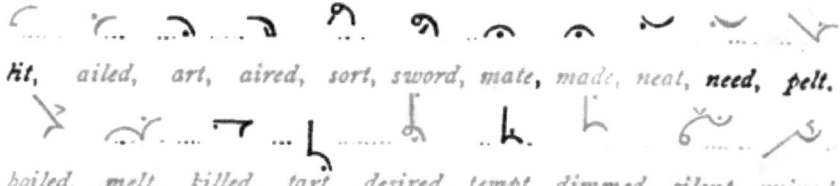

hit, ailed, art, aired, sort, sword, mate, made, neat, **need**, **pelt**, boiled, melt, killed, tart, desired, tempt, dimmed, silent, ruined.

3. The half-length stem for *lt* is written according to the same **rules as** full-length *La*, while the half-length for *ld* is invariably **made** downward, because it is *shaded*, and is vowelized the same as *Ya*—from the top down, because it is made downward, **like** *Ya*. Illustration:

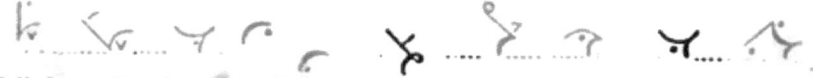

delight, polite, knell, lead, lad, puzzled, spoiled, mailed, nailed, revealed.

NOTE.—The vowel after a halved stem at the end of such words as *rated*, *righted*, *elated*, *avoided*, etc., is understood to be *ĕ*, therefore it is never necessary to write it.

ED TICK.

4. The syllable *ed* at the end of such derivativ words as *fated, sifted, remitted,* etc., where the primativ word *fate, sift,* etc., is halved to add a final *t* or *d*, is expressed by a small tick, written in the direction of *Te* or *Ka*, at the end of a word. Illustration:

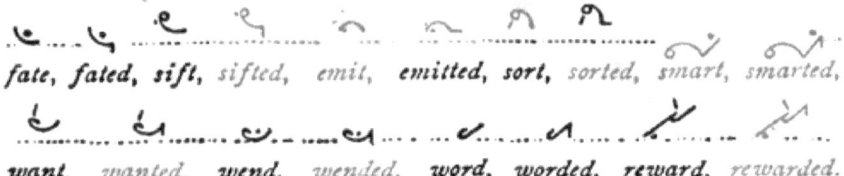

fate, fated, sift, sifted, emit, emitted, sort, sorted, smart, smarted,

want, wanted, wend, wended, word, worded, reward, rewarded.

5. The *ed* tick is also used at the end of full-length stems where it is not convenient or advisable to add the *d* sound by halving. Illustration:

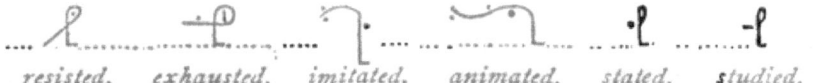

resisted, exhausted, imitated, animated, stated, studied.

6. The *ed* tick is written after the loops. When following the *str* loop it expresses only *d* with the vowel *e* omitted- Illustration:

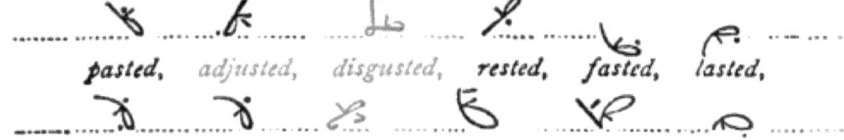

pasted, adjusted, disgusted, rested, fasted, lasted,

arrested, wasted, hoisted, fostered, bolstered, mastered.

7. The halving principle is very sparingly used in writing straight-stem words of *one* syllable; such words as *peat, pit, beat, bought, boat, bead, coat, cud, goat, guide,* etc,, being written by the majority of reporters with both stems, while others use the halving principle and never omit the vowels. Illustration:

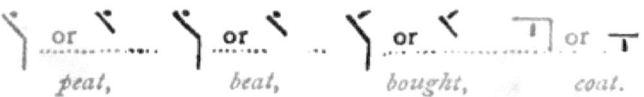

or   or   or   or

peat,   beat,   bought,   coat.

8. For convenience in speaking or writing, the halved stems can be named by adding the *t* or *d* sound to the stem name. Example: Pe, Pĕt or Pĕd, etc.; Ef, Eft; Ve, Vĕt or Vĕd; Ith, Itht; The,

Thĕt or Thĕd; Es, Est, etc.; La, Lăt or Lăd; El, Eld; Er, Ert or Erd; Ra, Răt or Răd; Em, Emt or Emd; Un, Unt or Und; Hah, Haht or Hahd. This will make distinguishihg terms for *p, t,* etc., expressed by *stems,* and *p, t,* etc,, expressed by *halving.*

9. *Ing, Wa,* and *Ya* are never halved.

10. The circle or loop on halved stems always read last. Illustration:

pets, sifts, salts, sorts, meets, needs, midst, didst, couldst.

11. The reporter writes *st* loop on halved stems to form the superlative degree of certain adjectives. Illustration:

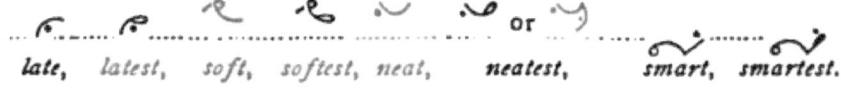

late, latest, soft, softest, neat, neatest, smart, smartest.

WHEN NOT TO HALVE.

12. The halving principle does not apply in the following cases:

(*a*). When initial *Ra,* in words of one syllable, is followed by *t* or *d*—writing such words as *right, rite, rate, road, rood, ride,* etc., with stems for *t* and *d.*

(*b*). When a final vowel follows *t* or *d*—writing *pity, tidy, duty, fatty, veto, muddy, naughty, lady,* etc., with stems for *t* and *d,* in order to furnish places for the vowels following the *t* and *d.*

(*c*). When the consonant before the *t* or *d* is both preceded and followed by vowels—writing such words as *abate, abode, acute, avoid, allayed, amid, unite; parried, borrowed, torrid, carried, furrowed, varied, married,* narrowed, harrowed, *pallid, tallowed, dallied, gullied, followed, valid,* mellowed, inlaid (La for *l*), wallowed (Wa hook), hallowed, yellowed (brief Ya), etc., with stems for *t* and *d.*

(*d*). When concurrent vowels come before the *t* or *d*—writing *poet, diet, fiat,* laureate, naid, etc., with stems for *t* and *d.*

(*e*). When *t* or *d* follows a stem preceded by another stem, with which it does not form an angle. Ilustration:

piped, bobbed, kicked, gagged,   liked,   fact, faggot, harrowed, reared.

13.—READING EXERCISE.

TERMINAL HALF-LENGTHS.

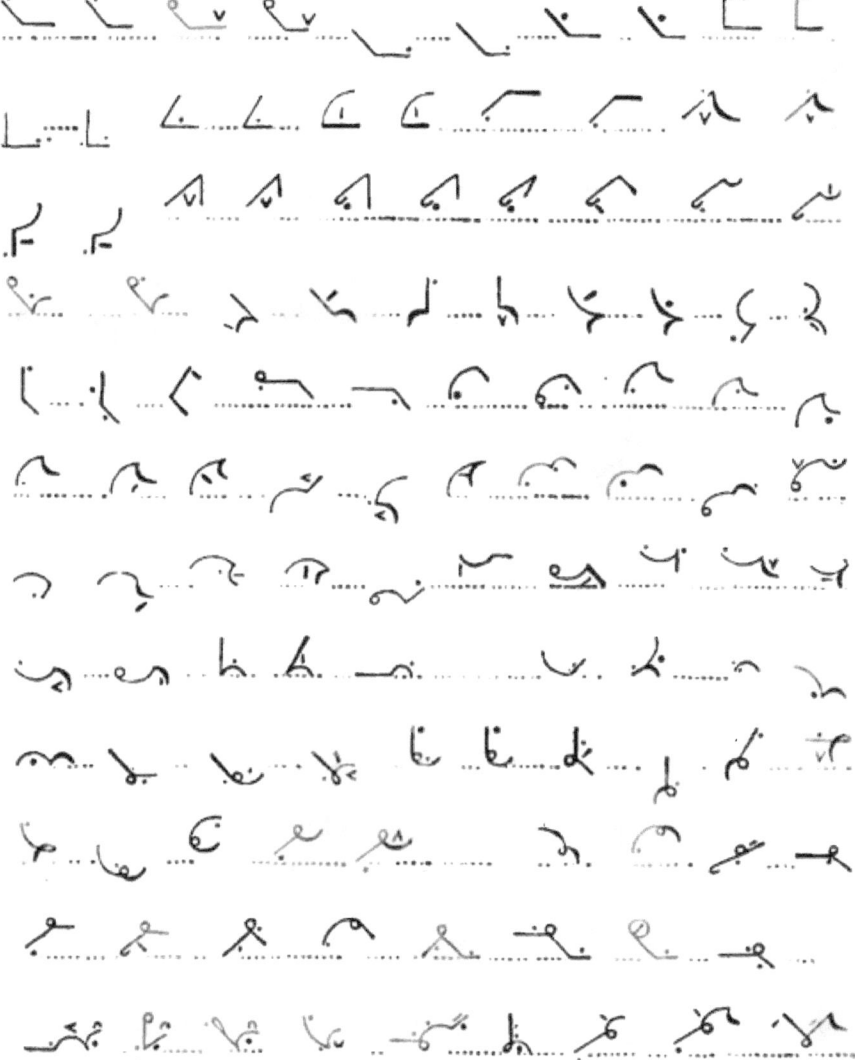

INITIAL HALF-LENGTHS.

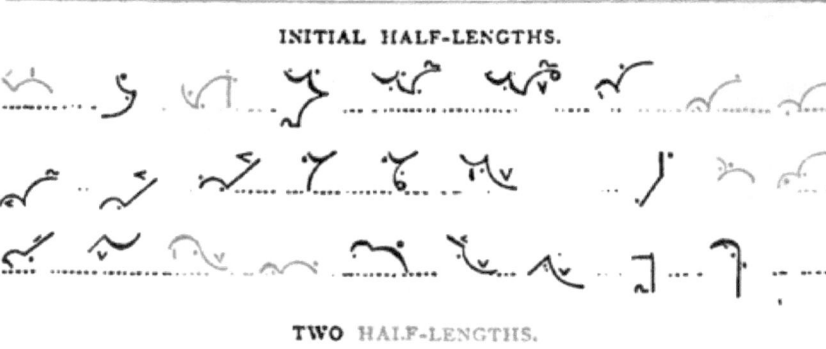

TWO HALF-LENGTHS.

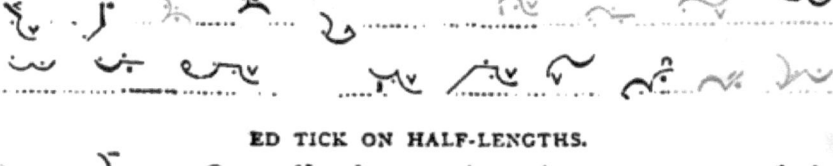

ED TICK ON HALF-LENGTHS.

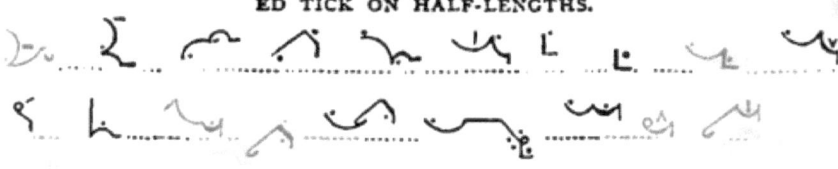

UPWARD ED TICK.

14. In writing the *ed* tick on *Lăt* it is better to strike it upward, on account of the liability, in rapid writing, of the downward tick becoming a hook. Illustration:

wilt, wilted, salted, related, emulated, diluted.

DISJOINED WHOLE AND HALF LENGTHS.

instituted, substituted, destitute, **pathetic,** emphatic, synthetic.

15.—WRITING EXERCISE.

Pick, picked, poke, poked, pack, packed, tick, **ticked**, **tuck**, tucked, tack, tacked, checked, joked, jagged, reasoned, **limit, remit,** limited, remitted, elect, elected, erect, erected, sift, sifted, **scent,** scented, sound, sounded, rescind, rescinded, resound, resounded, descend, descended, decent, descent, dissent, dissented, **absent, absented, invite, invited,** indict, indicted. repeated. reputed, **inhabited,** uninhabited, **remedied,** innocent

16.—ABBREVIATIONS—Half-Lengths.—No. 7.

put	issued	afterward
bad	let	forward
about	lead	inward
did	old, world	outward
debt	lord, read	better
doubt	might	debtor
caught	immediate-ly	yield
could	made	until
act	not	little
God, got	under, band, hundred	write
get, good	sent, cent,	written
thought	want, wInd	writing
that	went wont	
east	wild	astonish-ed
wished	word	establish-ed

17.—READING EXERCISE.

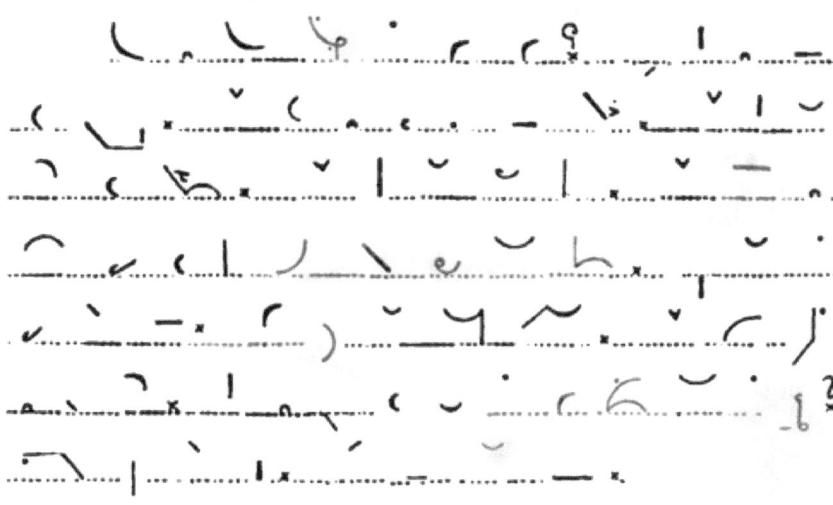

18.—WRITING EXERCISE.

You would enjoy a visit to the old world. I want you to give me your word that you will do all the good that lies in your power. Never go in debt. Read only good books. The Lord God leadeth me. We went to the woods afterward. Do not be too forward. That was a good act. He could not read for the want of a book. He is not a bad boy. Put your cap on the rack. How much good and beauty we have in this world! Have you any doubt about it? Put about that immediately. Go not afterward in debt. Doubt not the word of God. He went east. You had better go forward immediately. He could not get the goods. Did you get the writing? He was caught in the act. I thought you went afterward. He went immediately to let you know. That writing should be better. Yield not until the word is given. He wished he had issued that little writing. She went wild with astonishment. The debtor will not yield. They will take the lead in the old world. Might it not be written? He went when he was sent. I want to astonish you. One cent might be made to yield much good. Look inward if you would see how you look outward. Write immediately a little with your own hand. Better a hundred times establish yourself first.

INITIAL HOOKS.
LESSON XVI.

SMALL INITIAL HOOKS FOR *L* AND *R*, ON MATED STEMS.

1. When either *l* or *r* immediately follows any other consonant they are expressed by a small hook at the *beginning* of the consonant stem. Ilustration:

pl,   bl,   tl,   dl,   chl,   jl,   kl,   gl.

pr,   br,   tr,   dr,   chr,   jr,   kr,   gr.

fl.   fr,   thl,   thr,   shl,   shr.

2. In writing the hooks on stems, the first motion of the pen is made in an opposite, parallel direction to the stem; and the next and last motion is at right angles with the stem, as shown in the accompanying illustration:

Let these characters be practised with care until the hooks can be readily and perfectly made. Careless writers incline to make these hooks look like loops or circles. It is just as easy to make them right as wrong, if proper care is exercised in the beginning to understand the principles of movement in forming them.

L HOOK WORDS.

3. Notice that the *l* hooks are on the *right* and *upper* side of the stems.

plea,   please,   play,   plows,   able,   blows,   idle,   clay,   clause,   glow.

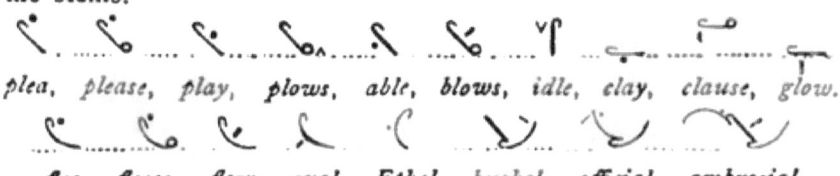

flee,   fleece,   flow,   oval,   Ethel,   bushel,   official,   ambrosial.

R HOOK WORDS.

4. Notice that the *r* hooks are on the *left* and *under* side.

*pry, praise, brew, **breeze**, **tree**, eater, trust, odor, draw, dress,*

*cry, **crow**, ochre, acre, grow, ogre, egress, grass,*

*freeze, frizzes, frost, throw, **ether**, **thrust**, usher, **azure**.*

5. In comparing the *l* and *r* hook signs, let the student regard

pl, tl, fl, thl,

and so forth, **as** so many pieces of wire bent so as to form the initial hook, and that these same pieces of bent wire, when TURNED OVER, become

*pr, **tr**, fr, thr.*

To illustrate still more clearly, let them be written in pairs, as follows:

etc.,

*pl, pr, bl, **br**,*

fl, fr, vl, vr, thl, thr, dhl, dhr, shl, shr, zhl, zhr,

—the *shr* and *zhr* forms being *turned over endwise* to give the forms for *shl* and **zhl**.

SPECIAL VOWELIZATION.

6. The initial hooks **are intended for** the expression of *l* and *r* **preceded by a** stem consonant without a vowel between the stem and hook consonants, as in *play*, *pry*, etc., and for the expression of such syllables as *ple*, *ble*, *fle*, *per*, *ber*, *ter*, etc., in *couple*, *bible*, *trifle*, *reaper*, *fiber*, *cater*, etc.; but there are many words of long, awkward form, such as *collect*, *correct*, *fulcrum*, *telegram*, etc., that are shortened in outline and rendered even more legible by using these hook signs; and for this class of words special rules, for showing that the vowel is to be read *between* the hook and the stem, are given.

7. When the vowel heard belongs to the *dash* class, represent it by the dash sign struck through the stem at right angles—made *heavy* for *long* vowels and *light* for *short* ones—and written in first, second, or third place, the same as in ordinary vowelization. Illustration:

fall, *cold,* *full,* *fulcrum.*

8. As the shape of the dots will not admit of their being written through the stem and be distinguished, like the dashes, the vowels of the *dot* class are represented by small circles, written, for *long* vowels, *before* upright and inclined stems, and *above* horizontal ones; written, for *short* vowels, *after* upright and inclined stems, and *below* horizontal ones, observing, as usual, the three vowel places. Illustration:

feel, *fail,* *carpets,* *fill,* *fell,* *paroxysm.*

9. When the vowels heard in *err* and *air* are to be read between the hook and stem, indicate it by making the parallel dash signs into ellipses, thus:

birth, *careless.*

10. The difthong signs are either struck *through* the stem, or else written at the beginning or at the end of stems, to denote that they are to be read *between* an initial hook and stem, thus:

cure, *casual.*

11.—READING EXERCISE.

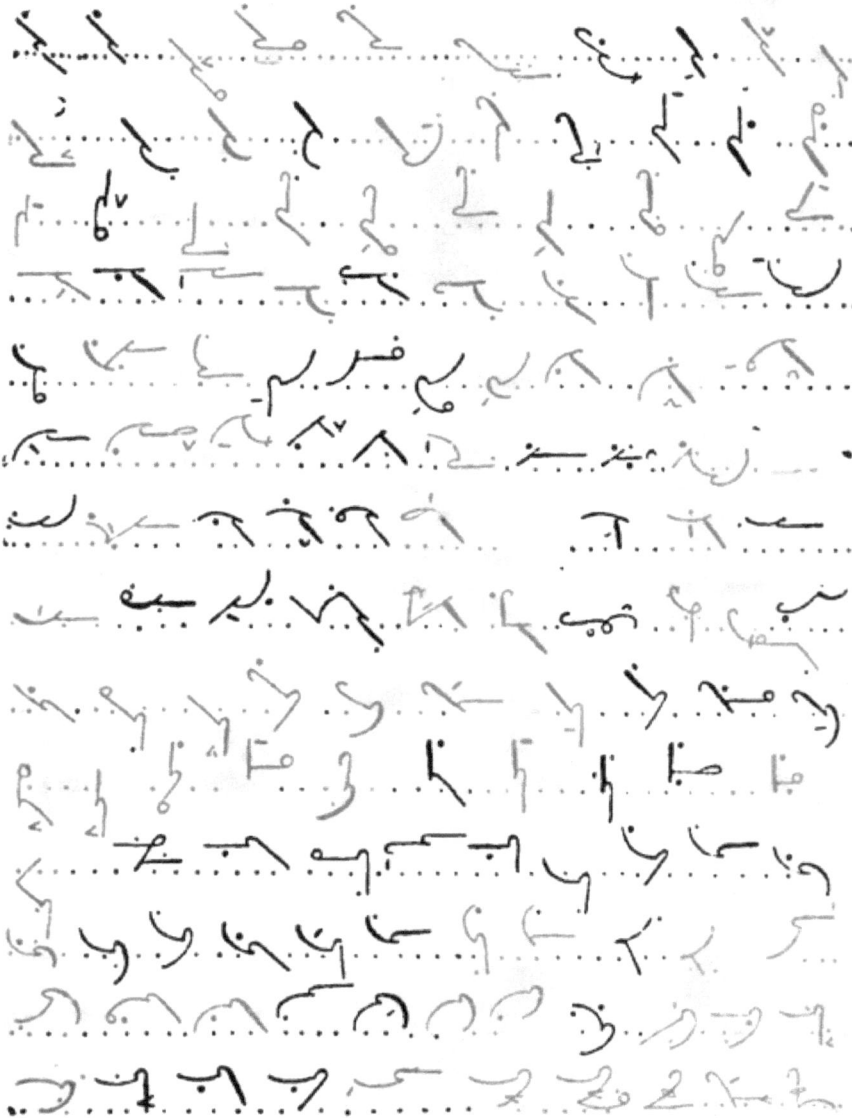

12.—WRITING EXERCISE.

Apple, able, ewe, eclat, please, pleases, pleased, play, played, plow, blow, blaze, blazed, idle, idles, clay, close, glaze, glass, fly, flow, fleece, flees, flies, flows, fleeced, oval.

People, peopled, pickled, buckled, tickled, cockled, giggled, fickle, cobble, gable, table, stable, stubble, scuffle, faithful, truthful, mouthful, treacle, draggle, prattle, brittle, scuttle, fiddle, victuals, thickly, flat blacker, flavor, pressure, special, initial, nuptial, impartial, impartiality, social, prudent especial, ambrosial, casual, visual, official, officially, bleach, oblige, club, cloth, clothes, clash, claim, gloom, youthful, vocal, unable, muddle, employ, simple, sample, example, dissemble, resemble, tumble, rumble, devil, level, lawful, ankle, uncle, angle, ethical, plaster, blister, bluster, cluster, cloister.

Pray, pry, brow, tree, trio, eater, try, utter, tray, draws, odor, cry, crew, acre, agree, free, fray, offer, offered affray, threw, throw, author, usher, azure.

Price, prize, prizes, prized, breeze, braced, trace, trust, trusted, crust, crazed, grist, grazed, grazes, grasses, thrice, thrust, precise, process, blazes, crisis, crises.

Prop, problem, prime, probe, approach, preach, pretty, bribe, brick, brag, brush, bravo, broom, broil, brier, briny, bridge, breeches, breath, breathe, break, bring, trip, tribe, trick, track, truth, trim, trash, drug, dream, droll, drear, dreary, drouth, dressy, creep, crape, group, grim, grab, growl, grog, frog, freak, frail, thrill, throng.

Paper, pauper, taper, dipper, cheaper, jobber, keeper, caper, copper, gutter, figure, vigor, vapor, vicar, entry, sentry, pitcher, major, lodger, ledger, archer, richer, Rogers, degree, decreed, degrade, sugar (Sha), shiver (Sha), measure, leisure, erasure, fisher, treazure, treasury, pleasure.

VOWELS HEARD BETWEEN HOOK AND STEM.

Germ, firm, Germany, person, charm, form, George, courage, fulsome, procure, cheerful.

L AND R HOOK ON UNMATED STEMS.

13. The initial hook for *l* on *Em*, *Un*, **Ra**, and *Hah* is made large. Illustration:

ml,   nl,   rl,   hl.

14. The hook for *r* on *Em*, *Un*, *Hah* is made *small*, and the stem *shaded*, **to** distinguish the *mr*, *nr*, and *hr* combination signs from *wm*, *wn*, and *Hah*, Illustration:

mr,   nr,   hr.

15. A large initial hook on *La* expresses the other liquid consonant, *r*. Let it be noticed of the two liquids that *La* takes a large hook for *r* and that *Ra* takes a large hook for *l*. Illustration:

lr,   rl.

16. The initial hooks for *l* and *r* are never **used on** *Es*, *Ze*, *Er*, *Ing*, or *Wa*. *Ing*, when hooked initially, being required to express *nr;* and *Es*, *Ze*, *Er*, *Wa*, when hooked initially, being required to express *Thr*, *Dhr*, *Fer*, *Ver*. *Yāl—Ya* with initial hook—is not used for anything, as it is an inconvenient form to join; besides, it is quicker and better to express *yl* by the *brief* **Ya** sign and *l* stem.

17.—READING EXERCISE.

camel, animal, canal, kernel and colonel, spiral, **exhale,** *help, color*

rumor, tremor, **moral,** *minor, north, cohere, adhere, inherit.*

18.—WRITING EXERCISE

Enamel, canaille, **kernel,** colonel, enameled, spirals, relapse, relapsed, relax, relaxes, **relaxed,** spinal, spaniel, channel, panel, canal, final, flannel, penal, vernal, finally, coral, choral, floral, rural, barrel, peril, Tyrol, plural, help, helper, helpless, health.

healthy, healthier, healthiest, healthful, heliotrope, halcyon, belm.
helmet, inhale, unwholesome, exhale, unhealthy, color, collar,
scholar, secular, Fowler, valor, **raillery**, stickler.

19.—*L* AND *R* HOOK ABBREVIATIONS.—No. 8.

R HOOK, STRAIGHT STEMS.

appear	true	larger
principal-ly, principle	doctor	care, occur
practise	dear	cure, accrue,
re-member	during	correct-ed
number	cheer	aggregate-ed
utter, truth	chair	agree,

L HOOK, STRAIGHT STEMS.

able, ably	deal	call equal-ly
till, tell	deliver	clerk
at all	children	collect-ed

R HOOK, CURVED STEMS.

form	either	humor
from	there, their	near, nor, honor
over	other	hire higher
every, very	sure, assure	hear, here, her
aver	share	hair
author, three	Mr., mere	remark
through	more	manner

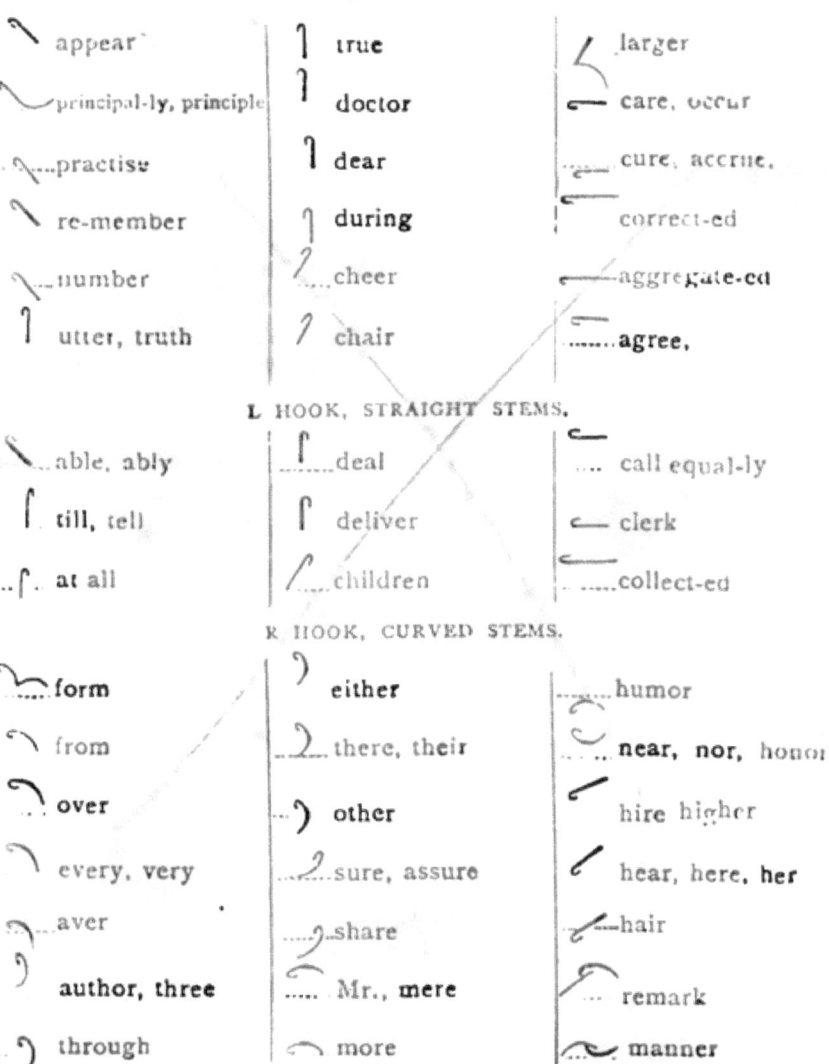

L HOOK, CURVED STEMS.

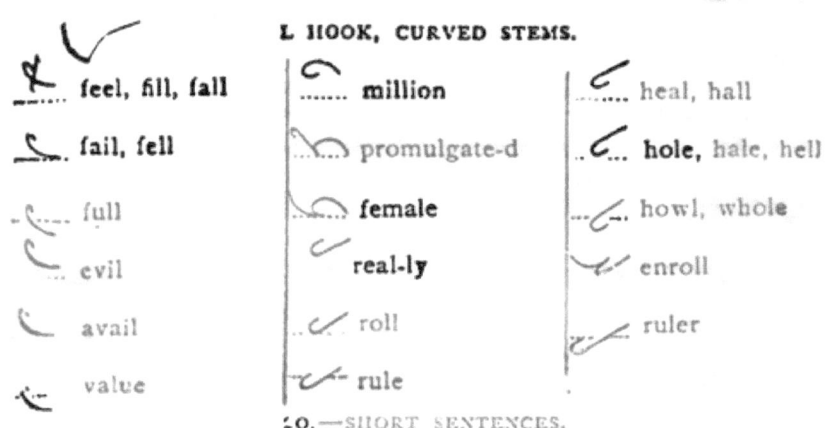

10.—SHORT SENTENCES.

I feel fully equal to the task. Practise the principle well. My principal imparts speed. Remember the days of thy youth, for thy very hairs are numbered. Utter only truth that you may speak with assurance. The principle thing in his address is humor. How ably the author treated the subject. I tell you, till all is well, take care. I have no faith at all. Form good habits if you would go through life happy, and from the path of truth depart not. Over all things honor is first. Every one knows his doctor well. Ever remember that *very* has a different form from *ever*. The author went three times through his book. Dear doctor, you cure and cheer; I feel you will heal a million. Put my children in the large chair very near here. To assure a cure you must deal with care. Either agree or take a smaller share. It will occur no more. How about the other, are you sure of the delivery? I do not remember the aggregate but the clerk could tell. Correct the clerk when you collect the fare. Mere humor is not more nor honor higher. Her hair was either black or gray, her eyes dear and true, and her manner equal. Did you hear the remark? I had my fill and feel so full I fear I shall either fail or fall. Ah, full well I fell! The evil did avail and its value I know too well. The female does really rule the family with a familiar hand. Hire a hall and promulgate the whole.

LESSON XVII.

THE INITIAL CIRCLE ON *L* AND *R* HOOK SIGNS.

1. To prefix *s* on *r* hook signs, the hook is made into a circle.
2. To prefix *s* on *l* hook signs, the circle is made *within* the hook. Illustration:

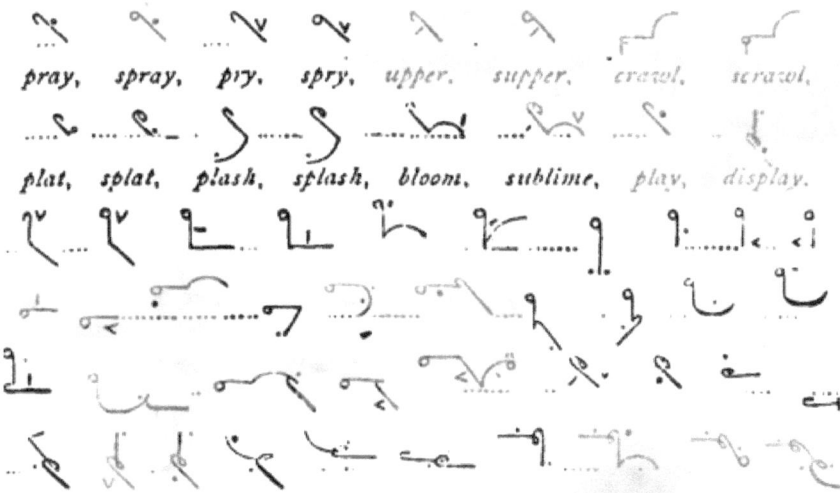

3. The circle on *Ka*, before an *l* hook on *Pe* and *Be*, is elongated or flattened, like a loop, and the pen is carried entirely *over the stem* before it turns to form the hook; thus enabling the writer to get that part of the hook, where it joins the stem on which it belongs, quite distinct.* Illustration:

excusable, explored.

4. In writing such words as *disagree, descry, prescribe,* etc., the circle is written on the right side of the first stem, and the second stem, which is *Ka* or *Ga,* is written directly out from the top of the circle. This brings the circle on the *r* hook side of *Ka* and *Ga*. Illustration:

disagree, prescribe.

---

* Some writers make the turn of the pen directly *on* the *Ka* stem, instead of after the *crossing over.* That way which is easiest and most legible to the writer is the *best*.

5. Many writers omit the *r* representation in the words *describe, prescribe,* etc., and express them thus:

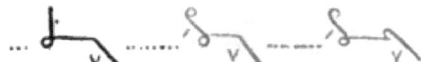

6. In writing the circle on the *r* hook side, *between* stems running in the *same* direction, it is not necessary to show the hook, as the *left* and *under* side of straight stems is known to be the *r* hook *side,* while the *right* and *upper* side of straight stems is known to be the *circle side.* Illustration:

psp, p-spr, tst, t-str, ksk, k-skr,

precept, prosper, dusty, destroy, distressed, cask, excrescence, excursive.

7. *Per* preceded by *Dis* is written thus; as in the words *disappear, disparage, dayspring,* etc.

8. In such words as **tasteful, boastful, trustful,** etc., where the *l* hook sign cannot be made following the *st* loop, the pen *crosses the stem,* thus reducing the loop to simple *s* and enabling the writer to form a perfect hook on the *Ef* stem. This contracts the words to *tas'ful, boas'ful, trus'ful,* etc. Illustration:

tasteful, boastful, trustful, breastplate.

9.—WRITING EXERCISE.

Spray, supper, sober, suitor, strew, cider, suppress, cypress, soberly, screw, scarcely secrecy, sacred, supply, sable, satchel, sickle, cycle, possible, disciple, display, displayed, accusable, physical, peaceful, passively, plausible, classical, classically, crucible, explore, taxable, graceful (the hook of the *Ef* in *graceful* is implied by the circle at the end of the *Ga* stem being elongated like a loop. If there was no *l* hook to express, the circle would be kept round, thus:). disgraceful, prosperous, prosperously, distresses, disaster, disasters, disastrous, **cheese-press,** Caspar, excreable, excursive, describe, disagreeable, disagreeably, disappear, disparage, dayspring, pastry, pasture (*Pēs-Cher*), extreme, gastric, mixture (*Em-Kās-Cher*), fixture (*Ef-Kās-Cher*), dishonor—

Straggle, struggle, strapper, supreme, soprano, sobriety, strata, stream, streamed, streamlet, strength, strangle, strangler, strangled, strut, street, strait, straight, straighter, sprite, sprout, sprayed, desperate, desperately, desperado, whisper, whispered, destroy, destroyed, distract, distracted, distrust, distrusted, trustful, distrustful, mistrust, mistrustful, expressly, describe, descried, prescribe, proscribe, subscribed, ascribed, abstract, extract, extracted, excusable, crucible, taxable, explore, explored, explode, exploded, display, displayed, displays, frustrate, frustrated, hemisphere (hemisfere), gossimer, moral, morally, curse, discourse, discoursed,

atmosphere immoral, mortal, immortal, course, persuade.

10.—ABBREVIATIONS.

CIRCLE ON L AND R HOOK SIGNS.—No. 9.

surprise	spread	supply
surprises	scare	supplied
surprised	secure	skill
spirit	scarce	scale
separate	scarcely	school

11.—SHORT SENTENCES.

I scarcely know what separated us. I was never more surprised. In a Phonographic school skill is supplied, but to secure skill one must scale the heights. My spirit is equal to the task but I cannot supply the energy. It surprises me that I have not surpassed others. Spirits are scarce about this place. He supplied the skill and she taught the school. The teachers were supplied with moral lessons to give the pupils through the course. The school-room was tasteful and the trustful teacher surprised by the spirit of the class.

LESSON XVIII.

BACK HOOK FOR *IN, EN, UN.*

1. The syllables *in, en* or *un*, preceding the *s* circle on *r* hook signs, are expressed by a small back hook, made so as to bring the circle on the *r* hook side of the stem. Illustration:

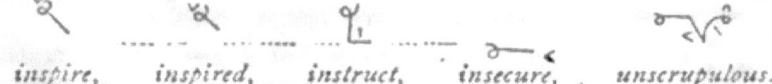

inspire, inspired, instruct, insecure, unscrupulous.

2. This hook is **also** used on *sla, ser, sem.* Illustration:

enslave, unceremonious, **unseemly.**

3.—WRITING EXERCISE.

Inseparable, inseparably, insuperable, unsuppressed, instructor, instrung, inscribe, insecurity, insoluble, unsolvable, unsalable, unsullied, insular, insult, insulted, unsolicited, unceremoniously, unseemly, ensample, ensemble (ongsombl).

4.—READING EXERCISE.—Sentences.

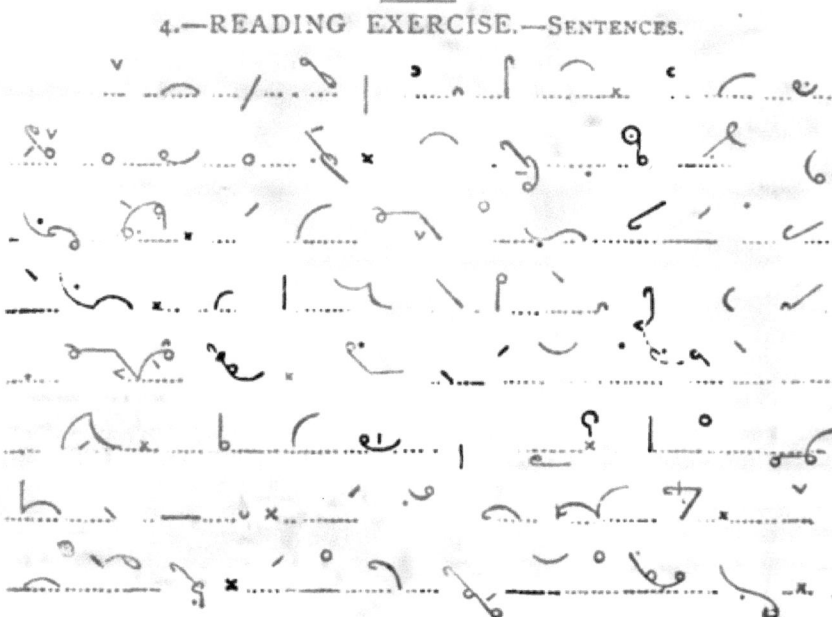

LESSON XIX.

W TICK.

1. The sound of *w* following a stem consonant is expressed by a vertical or horizontal tick joined initially to the stem. Illustration:

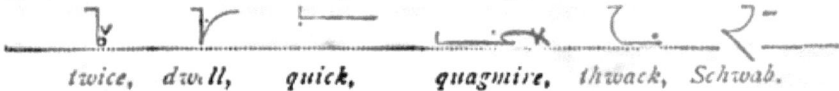

twice, dwell, quick, quagmire, thwack, Schwab.

2. Words with an initial *s* and medial *w* sound must be written with the disjoined *Wĕ* or *Wŭ* in its vowel position, thus:

squaw, squeeze, squizzle,

3. Words with *r* immediately following a *w* sound should always be written with the *w*-hook on the *Ra* stem, (*Wĕr*), thus:

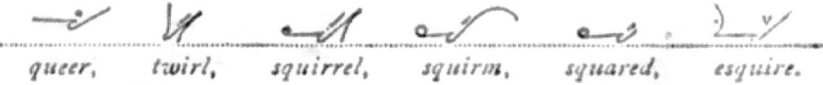

queer, twirl, squirrel, squirm, squared, esquire.

4. *Kwl* words must be written with *Wĕl*, thus:

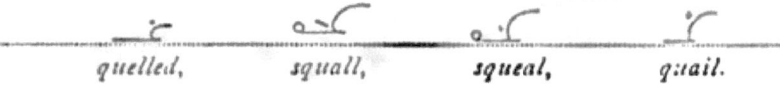

quelled, squall, squeal, quail.

5. The *Wŭ* tick is useful in writing such Spanish names as Puebla, Buena Vista, etc. Illustration:

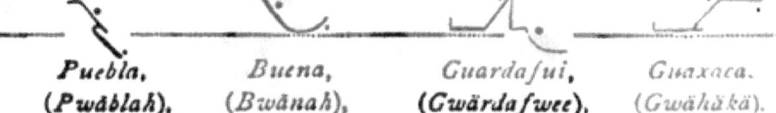

Puebla, Buena, Guardafui, Guaxaca.
(*Pwăblah*), (*Bwānah*), (*Gwärdafwee*), (*Gwähäkä*).

6.—WRITING EXERCISE.

Words to be written with the *w*-tick: Twist, twists, twisted, untwist, untwists, untwisted, tweezers, twitter, twinkle, twilight, twill, twilled, dwell, dwelt, Dwight, dweller, equip, equipoise, quibble, quiet, **quota**, quest, bequest, bequeath, quad, quick, quicker, quickest, quickly, quake, quaker, **quack**, quicksilver, quicksand, quagmire, **quaff**, quaffed, quoth, quiesce, acquiesce, quasi, quassia equator, thwack, thwacked, Thwing, Schwab, **Schwartz, bequeath.**

Words in which disjoined *Wĕ* or *Wū* must be used: **Squaw, squabble,** squatter, squeeze, squeak.

Words in which *Wĕr* must be used. Twirl, **dwarf,** dwarfed, dwarfish, **querl, quarrel,** quirk, queer, choir, **quire,** quart, squirt, squirted, **square,** squared, squirm, **esquire, query, quarry,** quarried, quartette.

Words in which *Wĕl* must be used: Quill, **quell, quail,** squall, sequel, squills, squeal.

LESSON XX.

SMALL TERMINAL HOOKS FOR *N*, *F*, AND *V*.

N HOOK.

1. The sound of *n* at the end of words and syllables, and in the middle of words where no vowel follows it, is represented by a small terminal hook made on the *left*, and *under side*, of straight stems, and on the *inside* of curved stems. Illustration:

pin, tinge, June, canopy, fine, loan, main, swain, run, hen.

2. S, terminating *n*-hook words, is expressed by making the hook into a circle, on straight stems, and by writing a circle *within* the hook of curves. Illustration:

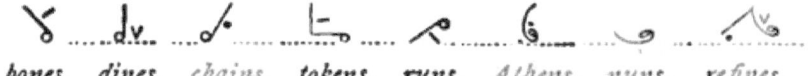

bones, dines, chains, tokens, runs, Athens, nuns, refines.

3. The large circle and the loops are written on the *n*-hook side to express *ns-s*, *nst*, *nstr*. Illustration:

expenses, enhances, danced, glanced, punster, spinsters.

F AND V HOOK.

4. The sound of *f*, or its cognate, *v*, at the end of words and syllables, and in the middle of words where no vowel follows it, is represesented by a small terminal hook made on the *circle side* of straight stems; and the circle for *s*, terminating *f* and *v*-hook words, is made *within* the hook, to distinguish it from simple *s* without the *f* or *v* sounds. Illustration:

proof, approves, devote, devise, division,

deafen, strife, gloves, archives, hoofs.

5. The **hook for** *f* **and** *v* is never written on the curve stems.

NOTE (*a*).—Observe that the *s* circle formed *within* hooks is elongated, like a loop, and made in the direction of the stem to which the hook belongs.

(*b*).—**The large circle and the loops** for *st* and *str* are never written on hooks.

6. If a vowel follows *n*, *f* or *v*, those consonants must be represented by the *stems*, in order to furnish a place for the vowel. Illustration:

brine, briny, fun, funny, assign, assignee, rain, rainy, cough, coffee, grieve, gravy, heave, heavy, rough, review.

7.—READING EXERCISE

8.—WRITING EXERCISE.

Fawn, pen, open, bane, bone, tan, eaten, **oaten, din, don, chain, chin,** june, coin, keen, cane, oaken, gun, gown.

Spun, spoon, sabin, satan, satin, stone, sadden, **scan, skin,** sicken, sustain, **Staten,** stewpan, weapon, widen, wooden, waken, wagon, worn, **Warren,** sweeten, Sweden, sworn, equestrian.

Prune, brown, **brain, bran, train, drown,** drawn, churn, adjourn, crane, acorn, crown, **corn, green, grain,** grin, groan.

Plain, plan, **blown, clean, clan, clown, glean,** glen, decline, recline.

Far, fun, vine, thin, assign, zone, **shine, lawn, urn, moon, nun.** Soften, seven, Simon, Stephen, Stamen, **flown.**

Suspense, strains, screens, widens, stamens, Stevens, woman's. Puff, bluff, pave, brave, strive, dove, cave, rove.

Puffs, **paves, drives,** chiefs, Jove's caves, **coughs,** cuffs, **graves, grieves.**

Panic, pancake, pinch, punch, punish, pennon, **bandy, banjo,** banish, tonnage, Channing, candy, conic, coinage, expunge, experiences, expenses, **finish,** (upward *sh*), **vanish,** heathenish, thinness, linear, lonely, minute, minute, minutely, minuteness, mental, mantel, miner, potent, potency, demean, organic, envenom, plenty, planet, plunge, blanch, French, fringe, penance, finance, synonym, sponge, Spanish, pippin, bobbin, obtain, Italian, deepen, detain, domain, **cabin, roughen, raven,** region, regain, famine, foreign, lemon, Lyman, remain, engine, tribune, blacken, **chairman,** African, Mormon, Norman.

Toughen, **deafen,** deafness, **define, divine,** devote, devout, devotee, devour, devise, advise, division, **(upward *sh*),** devotion, defence, advance, **extravagance,** extravagant.

Use upward *r*, Ra, in these words: Revere, rover, **river,** quiver, quaver, hover, cover, cleaver, clover, engraver, beverage.

Use downward *r*, Er, in these words: Devour, beaver, tougher, meaner, vainer, founder, finer, thinner, leaner, demeanor.

SHORT SENTENCES.

Ten honest men live in one town. Nine fair women spun sixteen **skeins of** woolen yarn. **The** moon shines upon the lawn. Green are the banks of Bonny Doon. When it rains, the Robins **say,** "Cheer up, cheer up, cheer up!" Rover is **a** brave dog, **you will** discover, and serves his master faithfully. **The** Bluff river divides **our farm.** Never swerve from **right** behavior. See the rainbow! The poor, with industry, are happier than the rich, in idleness. **Put down your pen and** join the children in their fun.

9.—ABBREVIATIONS.—*N, F,* **AND** *V* HOOKS.—No. 10.

N HOOK.

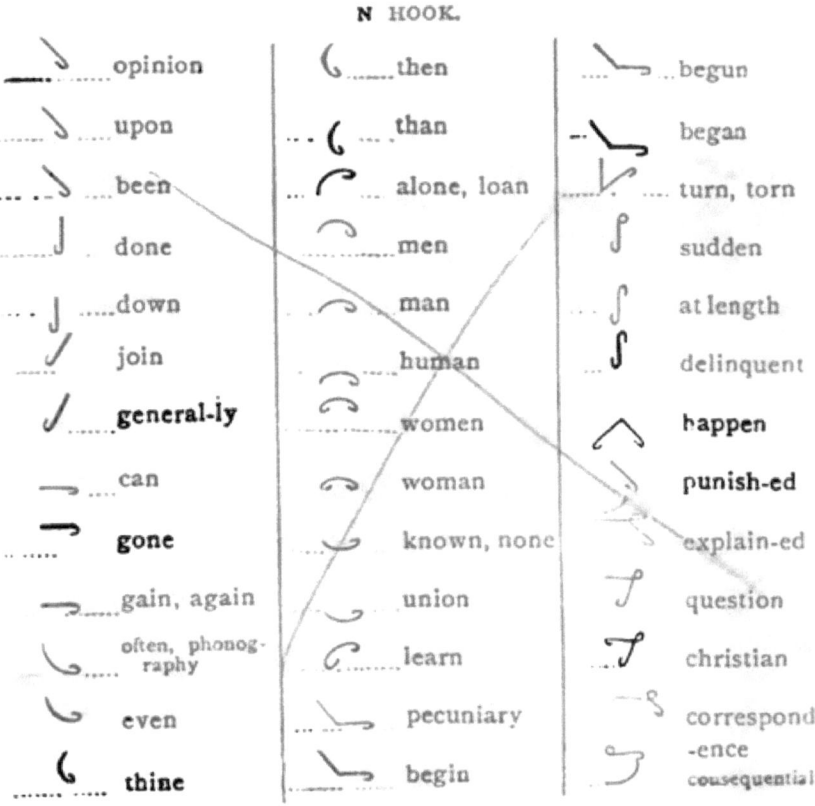

signify-ied-cant	southern	prudential
western	pertain	prominent
fallen	appertain	permanent

HALF-LENGTHS.

point, appoint	consequent	account
behind, bind	second	annoint-ed
tend	superintend	round
attend	acquaint	surround
did not, didn't	gained	around
do not, don't	find	understand
had not, hadn't	found	turned
gentlemen	foundation	accident
gentleman	land	subsequent
kind	mind	returned
can't	minds	learnt
cannot	meant, mend, amount	impend

ENS, ENSES, ENST.

at once	balanced	against
consequence	occurrence	indispensable
balance	Kansas	experience
balances	gains	transcript

F AND V HOOK.

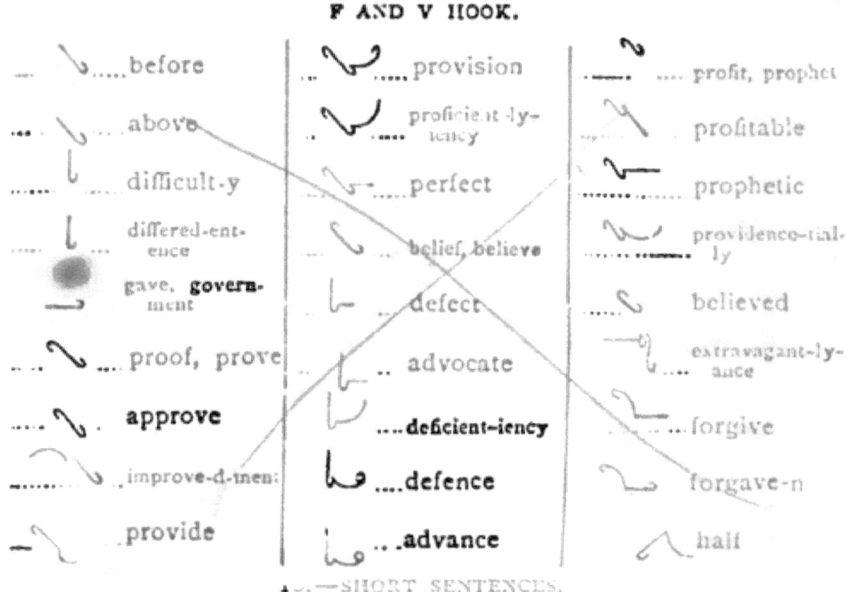

—SHORT SENTENCES.

Upon my opinion **I would** not **believe it.** Had it not been done **I would have joined the** general. **He could not** have gone so soon again! To gain **Phonography you must** first be found in a brown study; even then **it is best to be left** alone. Men are humane as women are womanly. The union was known to be complete. His pecuniary gain was not large. None but the good can explain their acts. Learn Phonography well. At length he explains the correspondence. The kind gentleman **did** not account for the accident. Don't go behind the returns. The superintendent found the foundation **turned** in consequence of the sudden accident. It is significant **of the fact** that he remembered that opinion. I find that the land **will** not yield a profit. His balance in Kansas is indispensable. He **meant to** surround the men but his general had fallen. The account was balanced with the amount. Experience is indispensable to understand the cost **of** success. He was punished but would not explain. Th occurrence in Kansas shows gains for the second time. **The** Stenographer's transcript was second to none. The advocate found difficulty in his defence. The deficiency balanced the account.

LESSON XXI.

SHUN AND ESHUN HOOKS.

SHUN HOOK.

1. The syllable *shun* (or *zhun*) following a *stem* consonant, is expressed by a large final hook made on *either* side of straight stems, and on the *concave* side of curve stems. Illustration:

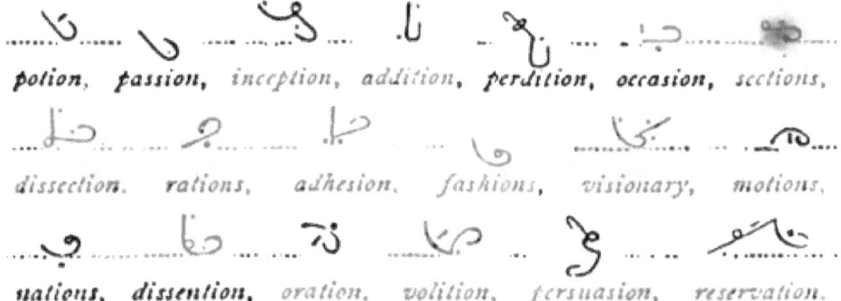

potion, passion, inception, addition, perdition, occasion, sections,

dissection, rations, adhesion, fashions, visionary, motions,

nations, dissention, oration, volition, persuasion, reservation.

2. In writing the words *unction, sanction, distinction,* etc., the stem for the *K'a* sound can be omitted, without impairing legibility. Illustration:

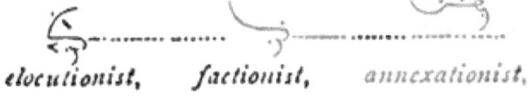

unction, sanctions, distinction.

3. The syllable *ist,* following *Shun* and *Eshun,* is expressed by half-length *Es* (*Est*) on the hooks. Illustration:

elocutionist, factionist, annexationist.

ESHUN HOOK.

4. The syllable *shun* following *s* represented by a *circle,* and a vowel, is expressed by a small hook on the back of the circle. Illustration:

position, **decision, accession,** physician, cessation, pulsation,

5. Words containing this small hook are legible without writing the vowel that is heard before the hook; but if it is desired to express this vowel any time, write it on the *left* side of the hook for a *first place* vowel and **on** the *right* side for other vowels. Illustration:

*precision,   transition,   **proc**ession,   sensational*

See Chapter XV. of Part II. **Text-Book for full** illustration of the *shn* representation.

6 —WRITING EXERCISE.

Potion, passion, passions, **editions**, addition, sedition, section, suction, deception, attraction, **attractions**, detraction, inception, subtraction, perception, reception, **ins**pection, exception, refraction, infraction, reduction, subtraction, perdition, approbation, attrition, reputation, selection, election, elocution, elocutionist, elocutionists, factionist, factionists, affectionate, affectionately observation.

Decision, causation, accession, accusation, physician, incision, musician; musicians, sensations, proposition, prepositions, supposition, cessation, secession, annexation; **a**nnexationist, pulsations.

SEN-HOOK.

The small hook for *shn* may also be used for *sn* in combinations where an *s*-circle and an *n*-stem would be inconvenient to join: It will not conflict with *shn* and will add greatly to speed and legibility. The principle justifying its use is the same as that for employing the *In, En* or *Un* hook—many final terminations being as inconvenient for the junction of *s* and *n* as for *n* and *s* initially. There are a few words in which the *Sen*-hook can be used medially. The following words will show its application. (See Part II., page 41.)

mason,   masonry,   medicine,   medicinal,   Wisconsin.

OFFSETS OR IMPERFECT HOOKS

Some combinations of consonants make it impossible to form perfect hooks; in which case it is necessary to make an offset, using a part of that stem (generally the second one) for the purpose which will make the best joining and indicate the hook; thus,

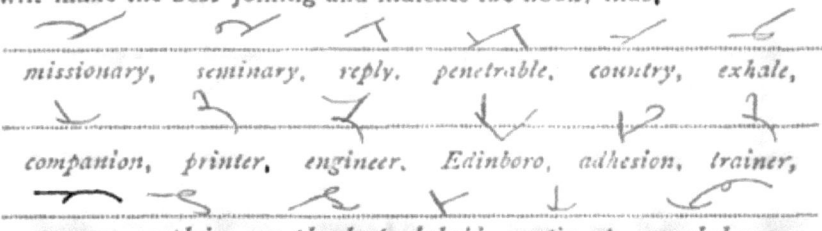
missionary,   seminary,   reply,   penetrable,   country,   exhale,

companion,   printer,   engineer,   Edinboro,   adhesion,   trainer,

economy,   explain,   resplendent,   behold,   continent,   unwholesome.

7.—ABBREVIATIONS.—Shun and Eshun Hooks.—No. 11.

SHUN HOOKS.

	passion		consideration		fashionable-bly
	objection		exaggeration		session
	objectionable		occasion		association
	subjection		creation		missionary
	exhibiton		direction		national
	tuition		correction		situation
	station		collection		dissuasion
	instruction		aggression		persuasion

ESHUN HOOK.

	opposition		acquisition		conversational
	position		procession		conversationist
	possession		proposition		compensation
	decision		generalization		civilization
	accession		organization		realization

SHADING AND LENGTHENING.

LESSON XXII.

SHADING EM.

1. *Em* is shaded to express a following *p* or *b*, and is then called *Emp* or *Emb*. Illustration:

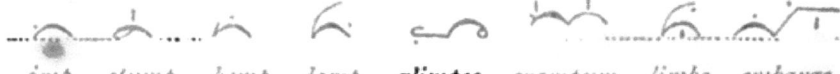

imp, stump, hemp, lamp, **glimpse,** wampum, limbo, embargo.

LENGTHENING EMP.

2. *Emp* is lengthened to add a following *r*. Illustration:

empire, temper, **simper,** ember, chamber, **somber.**

3.—WRITING EXERCISE.

Pomp, pum**ps, bump, damp,** dumps, stamp, stump, stampede, jumps, camp, **gump, vamp,** thump, lamp, lump, limp, romp, rump, mumps, swamp, **samp, slump,** hump, hemp, primp, plump, tramp, crump, cramp, glimpse, wampum, limbo, Jumbo, humbug, Sambo.

Pumper, Plumper, temper, temporal, distemper, damper, jumper, Kemper, vampire, romper, hamper, scamper, ember, umber, amber, somber, limber, lumber, chamber, slumber, December, November, September, dismember, timber, cumber, encumber, Cumberland, Chamberlain.

LENGTHENING ING.

4. *Ing* is lengthened to express a following *kr* (*Ker*) or *gr* (*Ger*). Illustration:

anchor **or anger,** sinker, winker, tinker,

thinker, finger, **linger,** stronger.

LENGTHENING THE OTHER CURVES.

5. Al' the other curved stems are lengthened to express a following *tr, dr, thr, dhr.* Illustration:

enter, render, smaller, mother, philanthropy, father.

6. Of the straight stems, only *Ra* and *Hah* are lengthened to express the following words:

writer, rather, hither.

7.—WRITING EXERCISE.

Anchor, sinker, Bunker, tinker, canker, rancor, ranker, linger, spanker, winkers, hanker, handkerchief.

Anger, finger, linger, languor, stronger, monger, mongrel, hunger, Hungerford.

Father, fatherless, fatherly, mother, motherly, motherless, thither, nitre, neuter, center, central, Easter, eastern, easterly. Esther, oyster, Astor, Astral, astronomy, astronomical, astronomer. latter, later, literature (*La-ter-Cher*), literary, latterly, literally, collateral, winter, wintered, wander, eccentric, eccentricity, render hinder, cinder, sunder, wither, withers, withered flounder. philantrophy, philanthropist, philanthropical.

Enterprise, interrupt, interruption, entertain, interest, interested. introduce, introduction, interpret, interpretation, interpose, intertwine, interdict, uninterrupted.

8.—ABBREVIATIONS.—Double Lengths.—No 12.

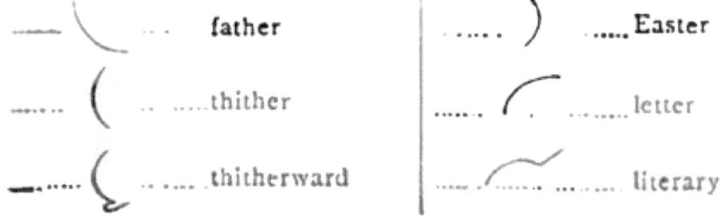

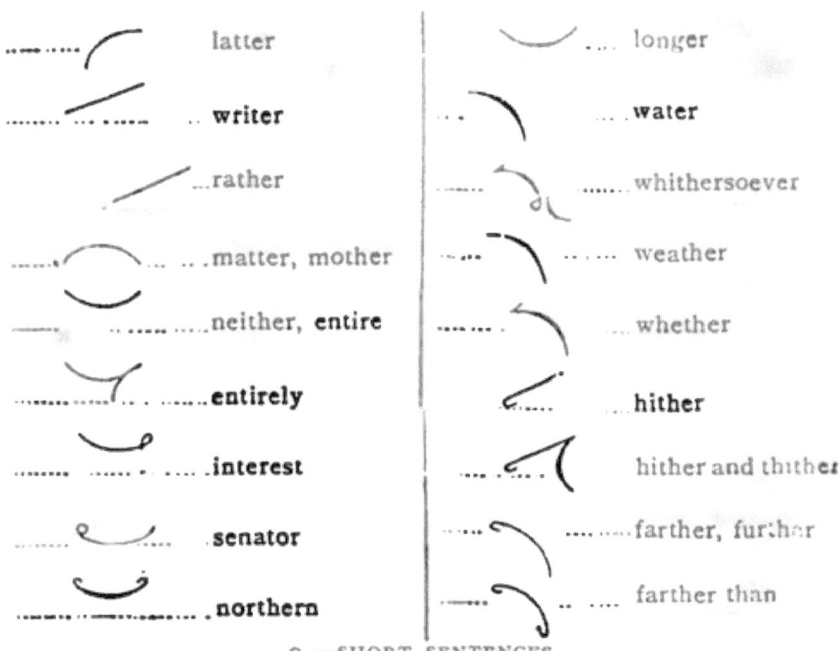

9.—SHORT SENTENCES.

His father and mother went thither. The style of the letter was literary. The writer wrote rather good matter. The Northern Senator went farther. His interest was entirely in the weather. Water no longer ran hither and thither. Father went farther than mother. I would rather be the latter. I should think it was rather longer than the other. It is better to go farther. Whithersoever you go, don't mind the weather. Whether the entire letter was sent by the writer I know not. My interest is entirely with neither. Your letter of introduction will further my father's desire. I hope you will not interpose an objection to the enterprise introduced. It was an interruption to intercept the letter.

PREFIXES AND AFFIXES.

LESSON XXIII.

PREFIXES.

1.—The prefixes, con, com, cum, cog; contra, contro, counter; fore; magna, magne, magni; circum, self; etc., are represented by brief arbitrary signs written either *before* or *above* the remainder of the word.

CON, COM, CUM, COG.

2.—The sign for *con*, *com*, *cum* and *cog* is a *dot*. Illustration:

contain, comprise, cumbersome, cognitiv.

CONTRA, CONTRO, ETC.

3.—The sign for *contra*, *contro* and *counter* is a *tick*. Illustration.

contradiction, controversy, countermand.

FORE.

4.—The sign for *fore* is *Ef*. Illustration:

forestall,

MAGNA, ETC.

5.—The sign for *maga*, *magne* and *magni* is *Em*. Illustration:

magnanimous, magnetic, magnify.

CIRCUM AND SELF.

6.—The sign, for *circum* and *self* is a small circle. written in *first* position *before* or *above* the remainder of the word, for *circum*, and in *second* position *before* or *above* the remainder of the word for self. Illustration:

circumscribe, self-made.

COMPOUND PREFIXES.

7.—Whenever any other syllable comes before these prefixes—thus making a compound prefix—the stem or sign for the syllable is **written** in the prefix's place, and the prefix is not written, but *implied*, or, *understood* to be expressed, together with the syllable standing in its place; or, in other words, if a stem or circle is written over another stem in such a way as to **occupy** the place of a prefix sign, it must be read together with the prefix—the syllable that the sign stands for being read first and the prefix last. Illustration:

conceivable, **inconceivable,** construe, misconstrue.

compromised, uncompromised, committal, non-committal.

cognition, **recognition,** conceit, self-conceit.

composed, decomposed, comfort, discomfort.

contradicted, uncontradicted, controvert, uncontroverted.

reconcilable, irreconcilable, magnetized, unmagnetized.

circumspect, uncircumspect, selfish, unselfish.

foreseen, **unforeseen,** accommodation, incognito

non-conductor, **uncommon,** concomitant.

8.—Some words, having the prefix *discon*, are not conveniently written according to the usual rules for writing compound prefix words, in which case, *the remainder of the word* is written *near* the prefix sign, and, in some cases, the prefix is expressed in full, about as quickly as to use a disconnected sign. Illustration:

disconnect.

9.—The syllable *kong*, in *Congress, conquer*, etc., is expressed by the *con* dot, thus:

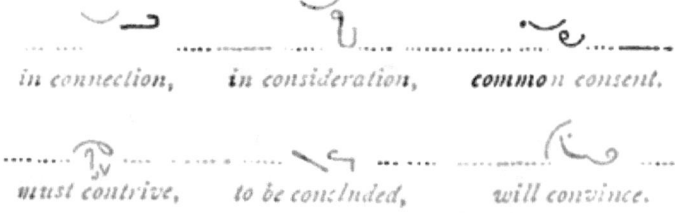

Congress, conquer.

10.—*Con, com* or *cog* can be expressed by writing the remainder of the word close to a preceding word, thus:

in connection, in consideration, common consent.

must contrive, to be concluded, will convince.

11.—READING EXERCISE.

common, commence, committee.

continued, constituent, contrition.

12.—WRITING EXERCISE.

Compute, **computed,** competition, compose, composes, composed, composition, compositor, compost, compound, compounded, compassion, comprise, comprised, compressed, comply, complied, complex, complexion, complication, complicate, combine, contain, **contains, contusion,** constrain, construction, contrite, contrition, con**tribute,** contribution, consistently, constantly, **continue,** continued, constrained, condemn, condemnation, conjure, concur, **concourse,** concrete, conclude, conclusion, **conclave,** conglomerate, conglomeration,** configuration, conflagration, convex, convivial, convenience, **convenient,** convey, conveyance, convert, convertible, conceive, **conception, completion,** compilation, compensation, condense, condensation, **contrive, contrives,** contrary, conduct, construct, contract, control, controllable, contrasted, console, consolation, consolidate, **consolidation,** conservatory, conservation, conservatism, concern, commune, commence,** commenced, conquer, conquerable, congress, congressional, **cognate, cognomen.**

Accomplish, accomplishments, accommodated.

Inconstant, inconsolable, uncontrollable, **unconvinced, unconquerable,** inconceivable, recompense, **recommend,** recommended, recognize, recognizes, recognized, recognition, recognizable, **misconstruction, miscompute,** non-conformity, non-committal, non-conductor, decomposition, **discomfort,** disconcert, disconcerted, disconnection.**

Contraband, contradict, **contradiction,** contradistinction, contravene, counterpoise, counterpoint, **counter-irritant, counter-irritation,** countermand, counter-mine, counter-balance, counterpart, **countersign.**

Join *f* for *for-e* in the following words: Foreknow, foreknowledge, forever, forward, forsake, **forlorn,** fore-thought, fore-handed, fore-noon, fore-fathers.

Disjoin *f* for *fore* in the following words: Foremost, fore-stall, forecast, foreman, foresail. See Part II., page 82, under the prefix *for, fore,* for a **fuller illustration of** this principle.

Magnanimous, magnanimity, magnify, magnificent, magnitude, magnetism, magnetic, magnesia.

LESSON XXIV.

AFFIXES.

The affix and prefix signs are treated and tabulated for ready reference in Chapters xvi. and xvii. of Part II. TEXT-BOOK.

The following frequently occurring affixes can be used to advantage at this stage of the study.

BLE, BLY—*b* with the *l*-hook when convenient to join, when not simple *b* will answer; thus,

tolerable, considerable-y, **indispensable**, profitable-y, sensible-y.

SELF, SELVES—a small circle for *self*, a large one for *selves*; thus,

himself, thyself, herself, myself; themselves, **ourselves**, yourselves.

SHIP—a disjoined *sh*; thus,

friendship, fellowship, partnership, generalship, relationship.

ING—a dot following the stem; thus,

owing, doing, **going**, cautioning, mastering, running, paying.

INGS—an oblique **heavy tick; thus,**

doings, sayings, blessings, **facings**, leanings, engravings.

INGLY—a tick or *l* written in *ings* place; thus,

lovingly, **knowingly**, seemingly, fittingly, trustingly.

FUL-LY—joined *f* when *Ef* with *l*-hook cannot be **used; thus,**

painful-ly, wakeful-ly, successful-ly, shameful-ly, youthful.

HOOD—*d;* thus,

manhood, womanhood, selfhood, sisterhood, neighborhood.

LY, AL, ALLY—disjoined *l;* thus,

manly, densely, instrumental, detrimental, sentimentally, shortly.

TO—thus, thereto, whereto, hitherto.

IN—thus, herein, wherein, therein.

AFTER—thus, hereafter. thereafter.

HAND—thus, beforehand, longhand, behindhand.

UNCLASSIFIED ABBREVIATIONS.

advertise	advertised	advertisement
adjust	afforded	actual-ly
accurate	accuracy	abbreviation
appear	appeared	appearance
appropriate	accepts-ance	after
anywhere	arrangement	always
arrive	anybody	anyhow
ask	certain	certainly
call	circumstances	calculate
clear	cleared	church
consider	considered	complete

All About Shorthand.

WHAT IS PHONOGRAPHY?

PHONOGRAPHY is the art of writing by sound. The sounds heard in a word are all that is written for the word. The alphabet is composed of forty-two letters, corresponding to the forty-two elementary sounds in the English language. The signs for the alphabet are selected from quadrants of circles, and from a straight line, written in four directions, instead of but one direction as in longhand writing. It is the simplest method of writing, and is adapted to all kinds of written communication, be it slow, as in friendship correspondence, or fast, as in taking the utterances of eloquent speakers talking at the rate of from one hundred and fifty to two hundred words a minute.

TO WHOM IS THE ART USEFUL?

PHONOGRAPHY is useful to every boy, girl, man and woman.

TO BOYS AND GIRLS as the greatest possible incentive and aid to education, and, ultimately, furnishing a pleasant and lucrative business.

TO MEN AND WOMEN in economizing time and in accomplishing at least a third more by its use than could be gained by longhand writing. Its study and practice quickens the intellectual faculties and disciplines the mind, giving the master of the art an advantage over those who have never received the intellectual benefit derived from the study of Phonography.

TO MINISTERS, who can compose their sermons with the rapidity of eloquent thoughts; many of whom also read their addresses from shorthand notes.

TO LAWYERS in making memoranda of legal points and testimony of witnesses.

TO AUTHORS in composition, being able to preserve their first thoughts, which are best, and accomplishing in a few weeks what would take a year's labor by longhand.

TO MERCHANTS in dictating their correspondence, telegrams, etc., to shorthand writers, thus securing promptness in business transactions.

TO STUDENTS, law, medical, or theological, in taking full notes of their school lectures, and by it helping to pay their college expenses.

TO ANYONE who may wish to make its practise a profession.

HOW SOON CAN IT BE LEARNED?

STUDYING from one to two hours a day for six or eight weeks at one's home will enable a student to write Phonography as rapidly as longhand is written, and this can be done by the aid of SCOTT-BROWNE'S TEXT-BOOKS OF PHONOGRAPHY, (advertised on another page), after which two or three months' practice, writing from two to four hours a day, from some one's reading, using for dictation practice, SCOTT-BROWNE'S Books of "Business Letters," will fit one for a position as amanuensis in a mercantile house. Lessons given by mail would shorten the time of learning considerably, and oral instruction in a College of Phonography would advance the pupil still more rapidly. For professional reporting it takes longer study, depending on the particular branch, or several branches of the practice, the student wishes to be fitted for. Some become only "Law Stenographers," others "Medical," "Sermon," "Literary," "Scientific," or "General" Stenographers, combining all the branches. The student generally fits first for an amanuensis position in business correspondence and then from that branches out into one of the kinds of professional reporting. Law reporting, to a certain extent, is the easiest to learn and generally the most remunerative branch of professional work.

WHAT IS AN AMANUENSIS?

THE amanuensis is a shorthand writer whose proficiency is only about two-thirds that of a law reporter; that is, his speed is from one hundred to one hundred and twenty-five words a minute, and his shorthand work is done entirely from dictation, in taking business letters from the manager of the correspondence department of business houses, banks, railroad offices, or letters or articles and books from authors and literary men. For which he is paid by the hour, day, week or folio. For rates, see Part II. Text-Book of Phonography.

THE PAY FOR SHORTHAND WORK.

AMANUENSES writing one hundred and twenty-five words a minute, possessing good educational abilities, receive in large business houses and corporations a salary of from $1,000 a year up. See list of graduates on another page for salaries they are receiving.

Official Court and General Stenographers receive salaries, or make by fees, from $2,500 to $5,000 a year. In some districts they do not make as much as these figures, while in other parts they make more. It is our purpose to keep within the bounds of reasonableness — unlike quacks who advertise only the exceptionally high salaries of stenographers, which are by no means a criterion as to the general prices paid.

Stenographers who can transcribe their shorthand notes on the Caligraph or other Typewriter receive larger salaries than longhand writers, because their transcripts are more legible, and by the help of the machine they are able to do two or three times more writing per day than with the pen.

SYSTEMS OF PHONOGRAPHY.

THERE'S no use in disguising the fact, as some teachers of the art endeavor to do, that there are several practical systems of shorthand in this country, all of them having both advantages and disadvantages, in some respects. There are, however, but four methods that have attained to the character of *general* utility, and they are

BENN PITMAN'S, the oldest system of Phonography in use, and the one having the greatest number of followers in America, but still a system that has not been revised or improved for nearly twenty years, since the practise of Shorthand became a profession.

ISAAC PITMAN'S latest modification — used more in England than America.

JAMES E. MUNSON'S completed "Complete Phonography"—and

SCOTT-BROWNE'S AMERICAN STANDARD, which brings down to date the best results attained by the Profession. It does away with thousands of useless "word-signs," contractions, arbitrary and illogical principles, used in other systems, and introduces simpler and more practicable forms. It possesses a series of text-books arranged for self or class instruction, leading the learner into full possession of the art by an easy, natural and graded method. It does away with confusing distinctions between "corresponding" and "reporting styles" of writing. And leads the student from the start into reporting knowledge and practice.

WHICH IS THE BEST SYSTEM?

REASON would dictate that that system was best that could be learned with the greatest ease, written the most rapidly, and read without difficulty. As most authors claim these advantages whether their systems possess them or not, the best way to arrive at a correct conclusion, is by the judgment passed by the writers of different systems, upon some one system, that one receiving the greatest favor. It may be seen by referring to another part of this circular, in which the opinions of stenographers are given as to the AMERICAN STANDARD, that the same has been found more helpful than any other system to the writers of different systems and necessarily must be the best system. It certainly has in its favor new principles for the symplifying of shorthand writing and the increase of speed and ready reading, that are not found in other systems, and which the writers of other systems adopt readily upon first seeing them. If it were not adapted to become more universal than other systems, it would not be accepted by the writers of different methods as it is; hence we must conclude that it is the best system, at least it is the only one that improves with time, and which improvements are incorporated in such a manner as to not detract from the system as first published, because the principles upon which it has been developed are founded in science and logic, differing in this respect from the other systems. But perhaps the strongest evidence tending to show the superiority of the AMERICAN STANDARD is the fact that the writers of Munson, Benn Pitman, Isaac Pitman, Marsh or any other phonography can read it, while the writers of any one of the other systems cannot read any of the other styles owing to the arbitrary character or plan on which they are developed. The necessity for shorthand in commercial correspondence has taken the place of longhand writing and points to the fact that uniformity in writing Phonography is coming to be a business necessity, the system used for such purpose must be unmistakable as to legibility, and all stenographers admit that the AMERICAN STANDARD is pre-eminent in this respect and hence is the system for the masses, and the best for the numerous reasons mentioned.

Read the commendations of eminent stenographers on another page

WHAT SYSTEM WOULD IT BE BEST TO LEARN?

IT WOULD be best to learn that system that is in most general use among professional reporters. It may be asked why? There are several reasons; the most important is that a great deal of correspondence is being conducted in shorthand characters. The time lost in transcribing can be saved to business men if correspondence can be done in shorthand so as to be as readily deciphered by the the receiver as by the sender of a shorthand letter. That system which is most used by reporters will become the one on which thru business necessities the business world will unite and use as its standard. The American Congress is reported by a corps of stenographers, any one of whom can read the notes of the others, so that in case of accident by sickness or otherwise, one reporter can take the work of another and transcribe it. The reporters by the AMERICAN STANDARD system, which is founded on the same plan of logical consistency and simplicity that is used by the Congressional Reporters, read each other's notes with the same facility, and as this method is the simplified and improved Benn Pitman style, and is the oldest system practised, and necessarily the one used by the large majority of professionals, it is the best system for the student to adopt as his standard. Uniformity in shorthand writing has more advantages than can be enumerated in this connection. When this condition is reached, shorthand will be in as general use as longhand is to-day, and the only thing that keeps it from becoming as popular is the wrangle of system makers, who will not work to this end, but labor only for the selfish purpose of a little fame and less money in projecting systems of ephemeral duration. Again, all systems except the AMERICAN STANDARD are so arbitrarily constructed that no two writers of any one of them writes in uniformity with any other. The principles are so arbitrary, the devices and contractions so complicated that practioners vary in their choice of writing words, and so find it difficult to read each other's notes. The AMERICAN STANDARD is founded and carried out upon a plan of simplicity and analogy, avoiding arbitrary and illogical methods, so that all can write it with perfect uniformity, and gain with it the highest results attained in shorthand reporting.

HOW TEACHING IS DONE.

BEGINNERS are taught the system most in use in this country; while students of any of the other systems are advanced into reporting practise by the systems they have studied. All instruction is imparted by dictation, in the very manner the art will be employed when learned. There is no dull, uninteresting routine of reciting lessons. The principles are learned and applied by practise from actual dictation, and the pupil is made as ready in reading his notes as in writing them.

Pupils are invited to spend their entire time at the College during business hours, in practise in reading their notes, and writing with each other, when not engaged in classes, or practising typewriting for a change or rest.

Lessons may be taken at the rate of one, two, three, four or five a week, day-time or evening, by mail or orally, as the pupil finds most convenient. The student makes the best progress on three lessons a week if he has only a portion of his time to study. Those having command of the entire time do best by taking five or six lessons a week.

SPECIAL OPPORTUNITIES.

THE POPULARITY attained by the College, together with the success achieved by it in obtaining positions for graduates, have attracted the attention of business men and those in need of stenographic help, who are almost daily applying to us for stenographers. Competent pupils are favored with reporting of this kind, for which they receive the full rates paid the profession.

Thru the efforts of Mr. Scott-Browne's BUREAU stenographers are constantly being sent to all parts of the country to take dictations or report Congressional and other Committees, Conventions, Boards, Literary Societies, Business Meetings, Political Speeches, Associations, Trials, etc., etc.

Besides these opportunities for pupils doing actual work, those who learn to operate a typewriter (see description on another page) are taken into our business office and trained in writing business letters from dictation and transcribing them on the machine, thus gaining actual business experience.

TIME REQUIRED TO GRADUATE.

A THREE months' course in the study of shorthand alone is generally sufficient to fit for amanuensis' work of moderate requirements. Some students remain in the College longer and attain higher proficiency, obtaining thereby a better position and larger salary.

LESSONS BY MAIL.

FOR information as to how lessons are given successfully thru the mail write us on the subject. We have developed the most successful method of giving instruction by mail now in use; many graduates, as may be seen on another page, having mastered the art thoroly by such lessons and are now in remunerative shorthand positions.

TYPEWRITING.

THIS is a rapid means of rendering shorthand notes into readable shape and is done by a machine made for that purpose, a knowledge of which is indispensible to the stenographer. Typewriting is taught in the Scott-Browne Chain of Phonographic Colleges, where the most thoro knowledge of Phonography is imparted. As an aid to the mastery of this little machine, which is learned in a short time, we would recommend Scott-Browne's Typewriting Instructor, a description of which may be seen on another page.

EXCHANGE OF BOOKS.

WRITERS of other systems who would prefer taking instruction in the AMERICAN STANDARD method and exchange for the books of the latter system, can do so at a trifling expense. It may be stated that other books that are to be displaced by the series recommended here will be accepted at one fourth their cost price.

TERMS FOR INSTRUCTION.

THE TERMS for lessons will be found on the last outside cover page of this pamphlet. We invite correspondence in regard to our school, board, etc., etc., which information we will be glad to furnish any correspondent.

CHAIN OF PHONOGRAPHIC COLLEGES.

THIS school is a branch of the Chain of Phonographic Colleges established by Mr. D. L. Scott-Browne, author of the AMERICAN STANDARD system. The purpose of Mr. Scott-Browne in establishing this chain of colleges is to confer benefits upon our graduates by his system, especially, and to help those who complete their courses of instruction by any other system in our school. Our graduates will, by request, if their application is accompanied by the recommendation of their teacher, have their names registered free of charge on the books of the Bureau for Supplying Stenographic Help, at Mr. Scott-Browne's office in New-York, and such persons will be shown a preference over all other stenographers in obtaining positions.

To persons contemplating taking up the study of Phonography it will be seen that this advantage, together with the advantage of writing the system most practised by reporters, will be found a very material aid to their success. This chain of Phonographic Colleges forms the only system of its kind in existence, and they are the only schools that not only take the pupil through the theory of shorthand, but also establish him or her in its practise, by watching the graduate's course continually, and recommending him for a position at the earliest opportunity after his graduation. It must not be understood however that positions are guaranteed, as the plan is simply to unite the influence of many schools with that of the popularity of the original school in New-York, and confer upon the graduates of our school the benefits of the combined chain of colleges. It may be seen how by this means a young stenographer without acquaintance or influence may have some one who has the power derived from such position to aid, recommend, introduce and plead his case, and help him to make a success of his undertaking. This is a benefit not conferred by any other system or school to one tenth the extent it is carried out in this strong and popular combination.

BOARD.

BOARD will be procured for pupils to suit their tastes, varying in price from moderate to dear, according to the style desired. By correspondence we could tell the exact cost of board. It will only be necessary for the student to call at the office of the College, or write, and state what he desires in board, etc., etc., in order to be suited.

MONEY MATTERS.

PUPILS' money will be deposited in Bank when desired, and drafts, checks or post-office orders cashed, thus saving them trouble and expense.

THE "AMERICAN STANDARD" SERIES OF PHONOGRAPHIC TEXT-BOOKS.

THE following list of works are the only books from which the popular AMERICAN STANDARD system of Phonography can be learned. They differ from other shorthand books in the following general particulars :

FIRST:—They have been prepared with special reference to the student's rapid acquisition of the art for any particular branch of the profession, or for general reporting. If a knowledge of law reporting only is desired, the Reporter's Book of Legal Forms and the chapter on Law Reporting, in Part II. Text-Book, will give all the desired information without hampering the mind of the student with principles, terms and technicalities which apply only to other branches of the profession. In learning the art for business letter writing the student is aided by the Book of Shorthand Abbreviations, the Business Letter Book for practise, and the chapters in Part II. on the Qualifications and Requirements of an Amanuensis. The Literary Reader and chapters in Part II. are for study in the mastery of the art for general or literary reporting.

SECOND :—Unlike any other series of books, each one of the set is in perfect harmony with every other one, and the lessons are graded from the simple to the most advanced style of reporting without a single change in phonographic outlines. All words used as abbreviations remain the same thruout the system, so that whatever the student learns in the beginning does not have to be changed to his utter confusion and discouragement as he advances, as is the case in all other systems to a very considerable extent.

THIRD :—No revision has been made of the system used by nine tenths of the reporters of this country for twenty years, till the introduction of the AMERICAN STANDARD series of Text-Books, and the art up to twenty years ago was founded only on theory. The profession of shorthand reporting has been popularized and has grown to enormous proportions during the past twenty years. To incorporate the new principles and improved methods of practise, as well as to present more concisely and clearly those principles that have heretofore been confusing, it has been necessary to revise the present work six times since its issue in August, 1882. It can hardly be expected that more than slight typographical errors will need to be altered in the books for several years at least, as it could not be expected that the art will change as much in the next twenty years as it has in the past; but if it should the latest revisions of the series will be in accordance therewith.

FOURTH:—In this system new principles have been developed that makes Phonography more uniform than it has been heretofore; preventing the unlimited amount of individuality in the formation of words and, necessarily, great irregularity that has been the consequence. By the principles of Analogy and Syllabication derivative outlines must correspond with their primitives and thus uniformity is established almost to a certainty. Take the book of "Abbreviations" which provides forms for all that class of words that are arbitrarily and of necessity written out of analogy, and uniformity is perfectly established, and that, too, by the simplification of the system instead of complicating it with expedients, devices, etc. By this plan the system is relieved of its unnecessary burdensome character which heretofore has made it such a herculean task to master: Now the thousands of arbitrary principles and abbreviations have been reduced to but a very few hundred.

FIFTH:—As may be seen by the appended commendations of professional reporters, teachers and others, this system is superior to all others and is the most popular.

In the following description of the books some more particular differences and advantages will be noted, and the order given in which they should be studied.

1—Text-Book of Phonography, Part I, prepared for the schoolroom or for the student's self-instruction. Presents the reporting style of the art in graded lessons, with reading and writing exercises; elucidating the theory in a clear, concise and fascinating manner. Is a perfect manual of the art. Price - - - - $1.00.

2—Phonographic Copy Book, No. 1, contains single and combined consonants and simple vowels with blank lines for their practise, and should be used with the above text-book. Price - - 25 cents.

3—Copy Book, No. 2, same as above with practise on the extra vowels, punctuation, capitalization, emphasis, dipthongs, joined vowel ticks, circles and loops. Price - - - - 25 cents.

4—First Phonographic Reader: Affords reading and writing practise on the reporting principles of the art as employed in a simple style of language, and gives lists of abbreviations at the head of each lesson, which occur in the lesson, so that when the work has been completed the student has had all the important abbreviations presented to him in reading practise, which is the easiest manner of memorizing them, differing in this respect from all other phonographic readers. Price - - - - - - - 50 cents.

5—**Key to the Reader.** Hardly necessary, as the Phonography is perfectly legible to any one who thoroly masters the principles in the preceeding books. This work is the popular Appleton Third Reader, and many may already possess it. Price - - 50 cents.

6—**Text-Book of Phonography, Part II.** contains forty chapters, illustrating every possible application of the principles to practise, with appropriate exercises for the student in confirming his knowledge for ready application in time of need. Chapters on the new principles of Analogy and Syllabication are given to illustrate their infinite importance in the practise of the art. Speed, or the Philosophy of Rapid Writing is treated in a manner never before attempted, and which will be found full of information and encouragement when the student attains that point where doubt and difficulty would be likely to discourage him. The qualifications and requirements necessary for reporting are explained as well as the conditions under which a stenographer works. Young stenographers errors are pointed out so that they may be avoided, business grooves indicated, equipments explained, and rates or salaries given. The work is an exhaustive treatise on the practise of the art, being unique in this respect, and the only book published from which such information can be gained. Students as well as professional stenographers of all systems require it as a book of reference and directions, general advice and instructions. Price - - - - - - - $2.00.

7—**Book of Shorthand Abbreviations** contains a complete tabulated list of all the "word-signs" or abbreviations of the system, together with a reference vocabulary of three thousand words in common use, words of peculiar construction, and words that have been written in various ways, establishing uniformity for the first time in any system; phrase-signs, longhand abbreviations used in business, and 400 names of persons, places, etc.; engraved in a style of the art never before approached for clearness and beauty. Bound in limp cloth for convenience in carrying in the pocket for reference and study. Price - - - - - - - - - 50 cents.

8—**Reporters Book of Legal Forms,** showing how the law reporter in taking testimony indicates questions and answers, objections, rulings of the court, remarks of the counsel, exhibits, etc., etc.: designed to aid the student mastering the art for law reporting, with key showing how transcripts are made out. Price - - 25 cents.

9—**Literary Phonographic Reader:** Prepared for reading and writing practise as an aid to the student in general or literary reporting, with nter-paged key. Price - - - - - 25 cents

10—**Books of Business Letters** form a collection of letters for dictation practise in gaining shorthand speed, and a knowledge of business terms and technicalities. The subjects of the letters are Dry

Goods, Agencies, Advertising, Brokerage, Collections, Credit, Insurance, Railroading, Manufacturing, etc., etc., covering hundreds of kinds of businesses—such letters as have never appeared in print before, and which have been collected with great difficulty from business houses. The dictation of no other work could be so valuable to a young stenographer for shorthand practise. These books are prepared in small and cheap editions to suit the convenience of purchasers. No student would need all of them. Most students would probably not need more than one, depending upon the class of work they would be required to do, or for which they were being fitted. The contents of each volume will show the character of letters contained. Those fitting for insurance offices would need all the letters on that subject, which would be found in Parts III. and IV. Agencies, Advertising, Brokerage, etc., would be found in Part III. and other branches of business in Parts I. and II. Below will be found the list of businesses represented by letters in the several parts already prepared. Other parts will be issued from time to time, till the subject of business correspondence is completely covered. They are bound in uniform style, in cloth, and sold at 75 cents per copy.

Part I. contains letters under the general head of Agriculture, on implements, vehicles, fowls and live stock. Under the head of Commerce railroading letters are given. Price - - - 75 cents.

Part II. completes letters on railroading, cotton and wool, oil and fuel, groceries and provisions, and dry goods. Price - - 75 cents.

Part III. completes letters on dry goods, printing and publishing, and gives, under head of Finance, letters on advertising, agencies, brokerage, collections, credit and insurance. Price - - 75 cents.

11—Scott-Browne's Typewriting Instructor. A work presenting fac-simile models of typewriter copying, giving specimens of legal forms, such as testimony, affidavits and summonses; specifications, business letters, bills, addressed envelopes, tabulated matter, literary and general work. A book that will be valuable even to typewriter copyists as a model for correct forms, and to the beginner invaluable on account of its graded practise exercise in fac-simile, which will aid to a mastery of the typewriter in a very short time. It is adapted to all writing machines, several styles being represented on its title page. Price - - - - - - - 50 cents.

12—Browne's Phonographic Monthly and Reporters Journal; organ of the profession, issued the 15th of each month, gives facsimiles of professional reporters' notes, with key, portraits and biographical sketches, phonographic news thruout the world, together with editorial and general discussions and the presentation of matters of vital importance to stenographers of all systems; unsectarian, untrammeled, fearless and vigorous, denouncing frauds and encouraging everything tending to advance the art, and aiding the student by good counsel and advice. Invaluable to any stenographer who is looking forward to the bettering of his condition. A sample copy free: 20 cents a number: $2.00 a year.

What Teachers and Stenographers Say

OF THE

American Standard Series of Phonographic Text-Books.

From B. M. JAGOE, Travelling Salesman of the Caligraph, 721 Chestnut Street, Philadelphia, Pa.

You must not fear about the success of Part II. It indeed supplies a want long felt by stenographers in general. I received the advanced copy in Pittsburg, and had many chances of showing it, and in all instances it was pronounced "The very thing that was needed." No shorthand writer, no matter what his stenographic creed may be, can afford to be without it. It is the stenographer's friend, containing a fund of information no where else to be found, and never before offered in any publication to the fraternity of shorthanders—a recourse to which may be desirable at any moment. It is a "gem" as far as binding and typographical appearance is concerned, being finely printed, every "hair-line" of each character "coming up" or "brought out" legibly, to the satisfaction of the most "Peter Precise" in the art typographic. I predict immense sales. All stenographers, both experts and learners, will be compelled to use Part II. as one of their "handy volumes." Have just sold my own copy to a teacher of "Longley's Ike," also a copy of Abbreviations. He is delighted with your books, and says if it were not for re-learning the vowel scale of position he certainly would teach his pupils "Scott-Browne." I meet many like him—the fact is, there is no system to compare with the American Standard. I had a talk with a prominent teacher of shorthand in this city, who holds one of the best paying positions in the place, during which he said he used your books in teaching "Isaac Pitman." He "could get better forms and outlines, besides ideas," which he "used to considerable advantage."

From THEO. F. SHUEY, of the corps of U. S. Senate Reporters, Washington, D. C., a writer of the "Old Phonography."

I have carefully examined your TEXT-BOOK OF PHONOGRAPHY, Part II. Wedded as I am to the Old Phonography, I find in your volume *many new and valuable principles* which, if I were a young writer, I should be glad to adopt, as I regard them to be perfectly safe in practise. Prior to last year I invariably recommended Benn Pitman's Manual to those seeking information on the subject, considering that to be the safest approach to the Old Fifth Edition. I then became convinced that the system as laid down in your TEXT-BOOK, Part I, is *more legible and philosophical*, and changed my recommendation accordingly. Now that I see it so ably and fully carried out in Part II, I feel clearly justified in so doing. I would particularly commend to young writers the matter beginning with chap. xxiv., containing practical information which in my own case (having begun the study of Phonography when a raw country youth of fifteen) it took years to acquire.

From FRED R. GUERNSEY, an old reporter by the Isaac Pitman system, now of the editorial staff of the *Boston Herald*, in its issue of November 26th, 1884, says:

An event of note in the shorthand world is the publication of Part II. of Scott-Browne's TEXT-BOOK OF PHONOGRAPHY. The book has been in the author's hands several years, and represents his best work in the development of Phonography. Whether the user is a follower of his system, (which is a modification of Benn Pitman's,) or not, the book will be very useful. The chapters on writing in Analogy and Syllabication are good pieces of work, and are worth the price of the book. Valuable to the writers of all systems are the chapters on law reporting, newspaper reporting, equipments, rates and salaries, qualifications, requirements, etc. There is a great deal in this volume which beginners by all systems ought to know. Scott-Browne is progressive, and gets out of the beaten track to the benefit of his readers. His Text-books are models of neatness and excellent arrangement.

From GEORGE MCDONALD, in *Truth Seeker* (New York), of which he is one of the editorial writers.

Unlike most other systems, the American Standard has shown itself to be progressive; the author did not stereotype his first conceptions and put them before the world as the last word on the subject. Where he has seen opportunities for improvements, those improvements have been unhesitatingly made. These are not, however, in the direction of arbitrary signs and intricate phrases, but in the way of consistency and legibility, and involve a theory of analogy which, proceeding from an established principle, carries a word through all its forms without changing the form of the primitive. The gain by this method in legibility must be apparent to all stenographers, and there is no reason for fearing any sacrifice of speed.

From W. A. LAW, Official Stenographer and writer of the Munson system Spartanburg, S. C.

I am delighted with TEXT-BOOK, Part II. Having examined carefully half a dozen of the most popular phonographic text-books, I claim for yours, without fear of contradiction, superiority in comprehensiveness and clearness. But what strikes me most, and let me say that it takes a working stenographer to appreciate this fully, is the vein of strong, practical common sense underlying every principle you advocate, and the total absence of those artistic impossibilities which have often been a great drawback to your g r eporters. The chapter on Prefixes and Affixes is excellent; your treatise on speed is a valuable acquisition to shorthand literature. These are not half the good points which a rapid glance at your book has revealed. Charles Dickens said, in the preface to "David Copperfield," that he regarded that work as a father does his favorite child; as the father of SCOTT-BROWNE'S TEXT-BOOK you are the subject of the heartiest envy on the part of the fraternity. You should be proud of your boy.

From GEORGE R. BISHOP, Stenographer to the N. Y. Stock Exchange.

I have been interested in looking the book [Part II.] through so far as I have had time to do so, particularly at your peculiar use of the back hook following the s-circle, formerly used for *thn* after the *s*. I have no doubt that for convenience of adding the following consonant stroke there would often be a good deal of advantage in this employment of it; and the question of *easy junction* is one of the most important ones in Phonography—in compassing a difficult one a writer may get left three or four signs behind; and I am in favor of even sacrificing a principle of analogy, occasionally, to accomplish or secure these easy or readily written angles. I think you gain something, too, by appending, or inserting, right in the text, in immediate connection with the explanation of forms and principles, of writing exercises. I observed that you had come round to the use that Mr. Eugene Davis and myself have for years made of the *h*-tick for *him*, as well as *he* and *the*. I am much pleased with the sign myself. I began to use it for *him* shortly before Mr. Davis did, I believe, and we came to the use of it, probably, from independent reasoning on the subject. My reasoning was this: if the sign for *who* is good for both *who* and *whom* why not the *h*-tick for both nominative and objective.

From JOHN W. BILLING, East Saginaw, Mich., Stenographer to the law firm of Tarsney & Weadock.

Shorthand Abbreviations and Parts I. and II. of the TEXT-BOOK OF PHONOGRAPHY are at hand. In your Abbreviations I find many improvements which, in my judgment, will apply to defects heretofore observed in Pitman's and Graham's methods. The opportunity for forming derivatives is excellent. There were many outlines written before in which the derivatives bore no resemblance to the primitives. Your Text-Books are simplicity themselves, and ought to be in the hands of all who desire to study the art, as well as those who have already mastered it. They do do not go into the redundancy so much observed in other works of like character.

From CHARLES C. MIDWOOD, Mechanicville, N. Y., an old practical Shorthand writer by the Pitman-Graham method, and Stenographer to the Gen. Man. of the Boston, Hoosac Tunnel & Western R. R.

I have read your Part II. TEXT-BOOK through from the first page to the last and think so well of it that I have gone back to first principles, and am *studying* it very *thoroughly*. I have adopted almost all of the abbreviations in the Book of Abbreviations and find they come quite readily Many of the outlines are longer than Pitman's, but after practising them I find they can be written quite as rapidly and read much easier. The chapter on Syllabication is one that cannot fail to be appreciated by all shorthand writers. I have no doubt that many writers, as well as myself, have sometimes found stumbling-blocks in many words ending in the *tion* syllable, which now can be very readily overcome. I cannot too highly recommend the book, and shall hereafter recommend it to all students I may teach.

From C. C. BRENNEMAN, Stenographer to the Georgia Pacific Railway Co., Birmingham, Ala., former writer of the Graham method.

I am of the opinion that you made the greatest discovery in Phonraphy that has yet been disclosed when you hit upon the principles of Syllabication and Analogy, which work together in the majority of words in perfect harmony, and I do not regret at all the two years that I waited for the single purpose of seeing your Part I. come out before taking up the art for practical purposes, and I only regret that I could not have been in New-York under your instruction when you were preparing your admirable Part II.

From H. P. WORMLEY, Quincy, Cal., Official Court Stenographer, by the Marsh system.

I am very much pleased with your TEXT-BOOK OF PHONOGRAPHY, and, although I write Marsh's system, I find many things in your book which I can study to advantage.

From TIMOTHY HORGAN, of Boston, Mass., Stenographer to R. H. White & Co.

TEXT-BOOK Part II. seems to be "just the thing." It anticipates everything that might be of use to the student or necessary for him to know, and gives a plain and satisfactory exposition of phonographic principles. I was very much puzzled in trying to understand the omitting of vowels in rapid writing, or rather, "the vowel rule of position," but now I have no trouble. I have received more for my money than I expected, and I would not part with the book for ten times its price.

From P. E. SWENEY, of Cleveland, Ohio.

Part II. TEXT-BOOK is just the thing I have been looking for for some time. Especially does it please me where you point out the errors which the young stenographer is likely to fall into. It seems to me that chapter was written for my special benefit, as several of the bad habits there pointed out I had already fallen into, but I trust that by strictly following your directions I shall overcome them.

From JOHN JACOBS, of Gardiner, Me.

I am pleased with your Part II. TEXT-BOOK, you have done splendidly in defining the laws and principles of shorthand to such perfection. You have Graham and Munson by the ears, and they will have no other chance for stealing improved systems.

From F. W. PIRRITTE, of New Market, Ont.

I am very much pleased that I have adopted your system, for with six weeks study I gained in speed several words more than I could write in Munson's system after seven months' study, and with *wonderfully increased legibility*.

From JOHN N. BRUNS, of Greenville, N. J.

I find the BOOK OF ABBREVIATIONS so valuable even to my system (Munson's) that I should not hesitate to pay $1.50 for it, if such were its cost.

From J. C. ROUZER, 1540 Chouteau Avenue, St. Louis, Mo.

The complete set of your TEXT-BOOKS came duly to hand, and to say that I am pleased with them is the very mildest way of expressing it. I am delighted to find them very small in size, but very complete in the text, and they certainly deserve the title of being a clear cut set of TEXT-BOOKS for the student desiring the best there is on the subject.

From P. E. and NELLIE M. BEARDSLEY, of Falls City, Neb., Stenographers to the First Judicial District.

Your MONTHLY is always a welcome visitor and is studied carefully by the entire firm. I estimate that the "Hel" and "Her" principles have been worth to us all we have ever paid for the MONTHLY from the first number. We have also adopted many labor saving forms from "Offered Improvements," which could only have been found in the MONTHLY.

From E. A. KILBOURNE, Stenographer to Manager of Grand Opera House, Chicago, Ill.

To criticise the MONTHLY would require a captiousness amounting to unfriendliness, and to withhold the encouragement and praise the work honestly merits, would be equally ungenerous. I can do neither, and by that I mean that I have no fault to find, and much praise to offer.

From FRED. R. GUERNSEY, of the Editorial Staff of the *Boston Herald*.

I was very glad to receive from my newsman several numbers of BROWNE'S PHONOGRAPHIC MONTHLY. I shall do all in my power to help on its circulation. *It is the best Shorthand Magazine in the World.* You deserve the thanks of the fraternity for your energy and keen appreciation of what the Phonographic world demands in the way of a bright and newsy journal. The fac-similes of actual reporting notes are invaluable.

TEACHERS' OPINIONS.

From REV. J. T. WARD, President Westminster Maryland College, Westminster, Md.

I have been very much pleased with your text-books of Phonography of which I have Parts I, and II. I am not a professional reporter, but I take great delight in Phonography. It is a scientific and beautiful art. The first text-book that I used was a little work published in New-York by Webster. I have also examined Benn Pitman's and other systems, but I have never met with any which I regard as good as yours.

From BROWN & HOLLAND, Principals of the Practical Shorthand School, 51 Dearborn Street, Chicago, Ill.

We have long desired a shorthand text-book with better arrangement than Benn Pitman's text-books have at present, and have eagerly examined each new work to find such. We are pleased with many things in your Part I., and have had in our school some writers of your system who have made satisfactory progress under our instructions, and we shall be pleased at any time to receive others. Part II. of your TEXT-BOOK is a guide to reporting in the fullest sense of the term. We have examined your Text-Books, and are very glad to find that, while you do not claim a new system in Phonography, you have presented the Pitman system with but slight changes, in its best and most complete form. We are satisfied that writers of every system will find in your book much that is valuable and of assistance to every earnest shorthander in reaching the goal of his ambition—a more thorough practise of shorthand writing and reading.

From W. H. WHEELER, in the *Auburn Daily Advertiser*; Benn Pitman reporter and member of the editorial staff of that paper.

The Benn Pitman writers have brought to them something that is even *more philosophic* than that excellent system, and, at the same time, nothing which can confuse them in the least.

From LOUCKS, CARROTHERS & BALL, Proprietors of the Capitol City Commercial College, 119 State Street, Albany, N. Y.

We used great caution in selecting a text-book of shorthand for our College, and after many trials with various other authors decided to adopt D. L. Scott-Browne's. We found it to be the simplest, and still the most comprehensive and practical, of any which came under our observation. Confident that it will meet the demand of the class-room, we cheerfully recommend it to the public.

From J. E. SLOCUMB, Principal of the Phonographic Department of The Nelson Business College, Cincinnati, O.

I have carefully examined Part II. of the American Standard Series of Text-Books, and recognize in it the completion of a simple, logical, systematical, philosophical and practical system. You have already been battering at the wall of erroneous ideas which has so long enshrouded Phonography; but in this work you have reached the culminatining point: the wall is demolished, its destruction is complete. The chapter on Speed is alone worth the price of the book. It shows that speed does not consist, as is commonly supposed, in burdening the mind with useless, illogical, and hence, impracticable phrases and arbitrary word-signs; but in the systematic training of the mind and hand—the mind to photograph, as it were, instantaneously the words as they fall from the speaker's lips, and the hand to as rapidly transfer these pictures to paper. Your treatment of the principles of Syllabication and Analogy must recommend itself to all. The book is original in its plan, clear in its directions and philosophical in its teachings. The typographical appearance of the book is perfect.

From M. A. WALTER, Principal of School of Phonography, 91 North Pearl Street, Albany, N. Y.

I have been using Benn Pitman's Manual in my school in this city, but think I would prefer your book, as it has always been a hobby of mine to keep the root word in the derivative if possible, and that Pitman does not do.

From W. C. SPEAKMAN, Steeleville, Pa.

Allow me to compliment you on your truly valuable work. Your books are permeated with good common sense, an ingredient not found in excess in the majority of Phonographic books. I shall lay the old time works on the shelf and endeavor to improve my notes by following the principles of the AMERICAN STANDARD. I am a Pitman writer and have long since wondered why some one had not made a common-sense improvement on that once grand but now antiquated system. My wonder ceases when I review your books.

From W. F. FITZGERALD, Teacher, West Troy, N. Y.

I am greatly pleased with your series of text-books. I recently sold a set of them to a young man who took lessons of me in the Pitman system, and he expresses much satisfaction with the simplicity and uniformity of your system.

From N. I. CONOLY, a graduate under Graham and Teacher in his School.

I find many things in your Part II. that are valuable to students of the art. Its simplicity and explicit directions must be appreciated by every lover of shorthand. Mr. Underhill's chapter on law reporting is a model of terseness and amplitude of instruction which every student will do well to study.

From Lou C. HANS, Wichita, Kans., Teacher of Phonography.

I have a complete set of your TEXT-BOOKS and can say they are worth their weight in gold. I am sure I have gained 20 words in speed from the use of your Part II. TEXT-BOOK.

From D. P. LINDSLEY, author of Takigraphy, in his *Shorthand Writer*.

Mr. Browne is a teacher, and embodies his experience in teaching the art. He could not fail to make a work of at least some practical utility. Mr. Browne duz not claim to present a new system. He retains the old Pitman alfabet of the ninth edition, avoiding the inversion of the vowel scale, which made such a turmoil in England and America ten or twelve years ago, and which Munson and more recently Longley have adopted. Mr. Browne's presentation of the elements is clear and practical. The joind vowel ticks of Lesson VI are a good feature, and the joining of the *Oa* in *Oasis* by means of the

Wa sign is quite ingenious. He also gives a joind *W*-tick which is convenient. The work before us contains only Part I, and comprizes only the elements and principles of contractions, the application of these principles being reserved for Part II. Mr. Browne claims among other things the following distinguishing features for his work:

1.—A convenient order of arrangement—reading and writing lessons following the text.
2.—Simplified directions and rules.
3.—A clear analysis of the vowel elements.
4.—Positiv values for the difthongal signs (making them independent of position.)
5.—Following vowels joind to difthongs.
6.—Joining brief *W* and *Y* almost invariably initially and medially.
7.—Vowels preceding or following the brief *W* or *Y* exprest by joind signs.
8.—Simplifying the writing of *H*.
9.—Changing Conflicting and illegible word-signs.
10.—Reducing their number from six thousand to about five hundred.
11.—Sparing use of the halving principle.
12.—Improving the prefix signs.

These improvements are all apparently in the right direction and aim at securing advantages for Fonografy. We think that Browne has made a useful work, and one that those determind to adhere to the old Fonografy wil do wel to study.

PRESS' OPINIONS.

From the *American Bookseller*, April 2nd, 1883.

Scott-Browne's Text Book of Phonography is the most concise work upon this art that has been brought before our notice.

From the *Norristown Herald*, Pa.

We have examined with much pleasure the Text-Book of Phonography by D. L. Scott-Browne; it is a complete and concise work and may be used to the greatest advantage by those intending to pursue the study of this subject, as it is becoming *the* system of shorthand.

From THE EDITOR of *Magazine fuer Stenographie* of Berlin, Germany.

The editor of the most favorite shorthand journal in America offers hereby in a very excellent shape and representation a text-book of Benn Pitman's Phonography, the principal system of Shorthand in America, augmented by such improvements as the author found practical during his long activity as teacher of Shorthand. Authors of German text-books of shorthand might consider this work a model in every direction.

From THOMAS ANDERSON, author and critic, London, England.

I should like to say a word about the Text-Book, and I shall say it as I have always endeavored to do in criticising shorthand books, guardedly and conscientiously. In the first place then, it is well and elegantly got up both inside and out. What to my mind, however, is of greater importance is this: that on a pretty cursory inspection I find it to be a more complete, elaborate and systematic presentation of Phonography than is anything of Pitman's from the great Isaac's own attempts down to the attempts of independent potters at his plan. I shall take any good opportunity I may be favored with to speak a good word for the MONTHLY as well as to give the Text-Book all appropriate praise.

From the *Notre Dame Scholastic*, Sept., 30, 1882.

This is not a new system of Phonography, but simply a new presentation of the old and popular system of Benn Pitman. The author of the new Text-Book, well known as the editor of BROWNE'S PHONOGRAPHIC MONTHLY, and teacher of the art of shorthand in New-York City, has incorporated in his work such modifications as during a course of eight years teaching, and in the practice by reporters by that method during the past ten or twelve years have been suggested and deemed worthy of acceptance. Many of these are valuable— one of them alone, the tick joined to the double vowel signs to express a third vowel, as in ro*y*al, tro*w*el, contin*u*ity, etc., is worth the price of the book to any stenographer. Scott-Browne's Text-Book professes to "discard many of the expedients, devises, contractions, word-signs, arbitrary and illogical principles found in other text-books and not found in the practice of reporters." Scott-Browne's text-book is a decided improvement over the Benn Pitman method of writing and offers many devices that will prove useful to writers by all methods. The lessons—24 in number—are admirably arranged in consecutive order and fully illustrated with engravings. The print is clear, on fine toned paper and the book is creditable alike to author and publisher.

From *Every Evening*, Wilmington, Delaware.

Students of the Benn Pitman system of shorthand, will find in Part I. a clear and concise, yet comprehensive, manual of the elements of the art as practiced by a large majority of professional stenographers of the United States. The author claims for the book that it embodies the improvements made in the last ten years. Whether it embodies all of them or not is probably a question upon which no two practical stenographers will agree, as each member of the profession almost insensibly acquires and adopts little pecularities and individualities which he grows in time to cherish, if not overvalue, but it can be truly said that if the student *masters* the lessons contained in this book he will need little but earnest practice of what he has acquired to fit himself for verbatim reporting. The author seems to have selected in the main very judiciously from the material in hand, adopting only such innovations as have been thoroughly tested in actual use. He has compiled his work, not from his own experience alone, but from the combined experience of leading phonographers throughout the United States, after extended comparison and investigation as to the best application of the principles of the art in their actual practice. A good feature of the book is its simplicity. The formidable list of word-signs in some other manuals is cut down to dimensions which can more readily be assimilated, the most serviceable among them being retained with a very few modifications which have been shown to be generally, improvements. When the advanced student has mastered these he can readily judge for himself of the advisability of extending the list, and, if he so desires, will be capable of doing so *ad libitum;* but the practice of the best writers has shown that there is a limit beyond which abbreviation, because of its tax upon the memory and its detracting from legibility, is not conducive to the best results in practice. Among the improvements adopted are the very useful *ed* and *w* ticks, the latter indicating the w sound as heard in "dwell," "quick" and many other words.

From the *Daily Times*, Moncton, N. B.

The Text-Book of Phonography, Part II. published by D. L. Scott-Browne, 23 Clinton Place, New-York, will be found a great boon to the brotherhood of Shorthand writers using the Benn Pitman system. It has been a matter of regret among Phonographers that the latter author has left his system just where it was a quarter of a century ago. Though ahead of every other system founded on the old ninth edition Isaac Pitman, it has not kept pace with the times, and the author of the work under notice, who is widely and favorably known in the profession has after long years of study and experience, adopted and perfected a number of changes, which we have no hesitation in pronouncing real improvements, and which tend to add both speed and legibility to the old system, besides rendering it more philosophical. There are many chapters in this work which will be found not only of incalculable benefit to the student, but which even the advanced writer can study with great profit, containing as they do a vast store of practical information which usually takes the expert Shorthand amanuensis or reporter many years to acquire in the active practice of the profession. The book fairly bristles with good points; its general get-up is beyond criticism, and is worth ten times the price ($2.)

A useful companion to the above is Scott-Browne's "SHORTHAND ABBREVIATIONS," containing a reference vocabulary of 3000 words in common use, words of peculiar construction, etc., and many other features of great value to the shorthander, be he professional or amateur.

Scott Browne also publishes the "PHONOGRAPHIC MONTHLY", an admirable publication which keeps the profession *au courant* with everything occuring in the shorthand world, besides containing much matter of value to those who are struggling with the mysteries of the art that "catches words and thoughts on the wing."

GRADUATES.

The following names and addresses of a few of the graduates by the American Standard will show what has been accomplished by students of this system. The salaries of some are not known, hence are not given. The brief record of each graduate's accomplishment will be found interesting and will serve as an answer to the questions: How long will it take to learn Shorthand, and what can I earn by it? The greater number of graduates were aided to their lucrative positions by Browne's Bureau for Supplying Stenographic Help, described on page 6, under the head of "Chain of Phonographic Colleges."

Mr. J. N. Blauvelt, of New Jersey, became Stenographer to Capt. W. H. Bixby, of the Corps of Engineers of the United States Army, located at Wilmington, N. C. Salary $100 per month. Mr. Blauvelt was formerly clerk in a wholesale Millinery store in New-York, at a salary of not more than half what he is now receiving.

Mr. W. L. Daniels, formerly of Boston, mastered Part I, Text-Book in 6 1-2 lessons, and wrote 125 words a minute correctly after three months' study. Is employed with the Mann Boudoir Car Co., of New-York, and receives a salary of $1200 a year. Was formerly a bookkeeper at a much smaller salary. Operates the Caligraph, and has found no machine to equal it for speed, durability and excellent work.

Mr. Stanley Gardner, of New Jersey, first practiced Law Reporting in New-York for a time, then accepted a position of $1500 a year as assistant Stenographer to the Corbin Banking Co., which in time he resigned to accept a much larger salary with the National Tub Works Co., of McKeesport, Pa.

Mr. George D. Hedian, of Pa., learned Shorthand during the vacations of the schools he taught, and became Stenographer to George Bancroft, the historian, at a salary of $1200 a year. He has been able to do the work required in his position and graduate at the National Law School of Washington, D. C. He spends his summers with Mr. Bancroft in Newport, R. I.

Mr. C. H. Larkin, of Tenn., completed a course in three months' time, and was placed in the house of Thompson & Bedford Co., in New-York at $20 a week. He was formerly earning half that salary as a printer.

Mr. Geo. B. Sheppard, of Brooklyn, N. Y., took his first position with the Indianapolis, Springfield and Decatur R. R., at a salary of $20 per week. Learning the railroad business in this position he was offered a better one with the Chicago & Northwestern R. R., and in time a still better with the Union Pacific R. R., of Omaha, Neb. Previous to learning shorthand, he was a clerk in a publishing house, at a salary of not half what he is now receiving.

Mr. John Ross, of Canada, a carpenter by trade, learning the art took a position in a large house in New-York doing business with Mexico. His letters were passed over to a Spanish Translator who was paid $1. per letter for putting them into that language. Mr. Ross learned Spanish within a year's time by evening study and received an increase of salary making the sum, we understand, of $30 per week.

Mr. S. B. Sheibly, of Ga., a telegrapher, became stenographer to Attorney General Brewster, Washington, D. C., at a salary of $1800 a year. He previously received $90 a month with the W. U. Tel. Co.

Mr. Geo. A. Taylor, of Indiana, was first stenographer to the N. Y. Central R. R. Co., New-York, and afterward with Cameron, Castles & Story, of Waco, Texas, at $1500 a year.

Mr. J. D. Hashagen, of New-York, became stenographer to the Savannah, Florida & Western R. R., and upon learning the R. R. business was transferred to New-York, and made Gen. Freight Agent on this and several other lines of roads.

Mr. Chas. E. Pennoyer, of Nebraska, with Scribner, Welford & Co., New-York, at $20 per week.

Mr. Jos. T. Brown with E. O. Bowers, Commission Merchant, New-York, $20 per week.

Mr. Geo. E. Plunkitt, of New-York, Stenographer to the Hon. John Kelly, President of the Tammany Society, resigned to accept a a similar position with Major Hull of the American Institute, and was afterward appointed Official Stenographer of the 11th Judicial District Court of New-York at a salary of $2,000 per year, and 10 cts. per folio for transcripts. Mr. Plunkitt is but 21 years of age, and had his choice when 18 years old to go to college or learn a business. He choose to learn Phonography, which has given him a splendid practical education and abundant remuneration for his time.

Mr. John F. Snyder, of Pennsylvania, first served in the New York and New England R. R. Co. in Boston at $75 per month, and in due time accepted $90 per month, in Lynchburg, Va., with the Norfolk & Western R. R. Was previously a longhand clerk in a railroad office at a salary of $50 per month.

Mr. M. A. Cohen, of Savannah, Ga., was appointed official Stenographer of the Superior Court of that City, which led to a thorough knowledge of law and being offered a partnership in probably the most influential law firm of the South accepted the same.

Mr. C. C. Brenneman, of Ohio, first took a position in New-York at $15 per week in a glass house and afterwards was advanced to $18 in a law office, and then accepted $25 per week with the Georgia & Pacific R. R. Co., of Birmingham, Ala.

Mr. W. P. Norris, of Richmond, Ky., graduated in three months, and became stenographer to H. S. Douthitt, Probate Judge, Howard, Kansas.

Mr. H. S. Jennison after four months careful study became master of the art and is employed by Venable & Co., the largest tobacco manufacturers in Virginia, and receives from them a liberal salary.

Mr. J. A. Shindell studied Phonography while preparing himself to become private secretary to the Secretary of the Philadelphia & Reading Railroad, but being limited to six weeks time in preparation, did not graduate, though he mastered the principles of the art in that time sufficiently to enter upon the discharge of his duties.

Mr. Geo. Malone of Washington, D. C., immediately upon graduating had his salary doubled by his present employer, Mr. Frank W. Hackett, 486 Louisiana Avenue.

Mr. Francis P. McGhan took a finishing course, and in a few months was able to take down verbatim public speeches, and performed some very difficult reporting for the Bureau of Navigation, Washington, D. C. He is a phenomenally rapid writer. Mr. McGhan is a mechanic and still works at his trade, and few reporters can do shorthand work at greater speed than he.

Mr. John McMahon, Jr., of Washington, D. C., learned Phonography as a part of a practical education. His father, Mr. John McMahon, of the U. S. Treasury, who is a mathematician by profession and a graduate of Dublin University, deems a knowledge of Shorthand essential to a good business education.

Mr. F. W. Moulton, of Washington, D. C., resigned a government position to become stenographer in the Washington Telephone Headquarters at a salary of $900 a year. He made himself so valuable to his employers that his salary was increased to $1500 within a few months.

Mr. Gaines Rice, of Burlington, Ky., gained 70 words a minute in two months instruction. He entered the college with 80 words and left with 150 a minute.

Mr. S. J. Stedman, of Cincinnati, gained 70 words in two months study; entering with 70 words and leaving with 140.

Mr. David Strauss, of Cincinnati, began the study and in three months time attained the proficiency of writing 120 words a minute, and was immediately made stenographer to the Railway Supply and Manufacturing Co., of Second Street, Cincinnati.

Mr. F. H. Vogt, of East Walnut Hills, Cincinnati, thoroughly mastered Part 1, Text-Book in eleven lessons, and wrote 100 words per minute after taking 30 lessons.

Mr. George Francis Train, Jr., with his knowledge of shorthand became teller of the Kountze Bros. Bank, New-York.

Mr. G. Edgar Allen, of Kansas City, Mo., with the Favorite Carriage Co., Cincinnati, Ohio

Mr. Wm. Harrison, of Maine, located in St. Paul, Minn., taking a position with a Railroad Co., at a **salary of $60** per month which was rapidly advanced to $150 a month.

Mr. George Lucas, of New-York, a dry goods clerk on a salary of $7 a week, after six months study of 3 lessons a week accepted a position in Washington, D. C., at $40 a week.

LADY GRADUATES.

Miss Josephine Campbell, of 600 F St., Washington, D. C., employed as shorthand writer and typewriter operator with one of the largest firms of Patent Lawyers in Washington, doing the very difficult work that shorthand writers are somtimes called upon to do, viz: taking specifications in patent cases from dictation.

Miss Bessie Cowell, of 1818 16th St., Washington, D. C., although but sixteen years of age, is a thorough master of Phonography. She is a granddaughter of Prof. Robert Phipps, a gentleman who has been favorably known in Washington for many years, and who regards a knowledge of shorthand as necessary to complete the education of a young lady.

Mrs. Louise H. Esselstyn, teacher in Hamilton College, Hamilton. N. Y., learned the Remington Typewriter in conection with her Shorthand and in less than three months study of the art, was able to take a position in a large confectionery supply house, at $12 per week. A few months afterward, was offered a place in the office of the Century Co., New-York, at a salary of $25 per week. In this position she was required to use the Hammond Typewriter with Greek type in preparing manuscript for publication. Her educational qualifications were appreciated, and she is now receiving about **double** the salary she formerly received in the profession of teaching.

Miss Alice Stanley Boynton, of Brooklyn, N. Y., a lady of culture and independence, learned the art for the sake of having an occupation; being for some time engaged in the Export Department of the Domestic Sewing Machine Co., she resigned this position to accept a better one with the **paper house** of Wilkinson & Brother, at $20 per week.

Miss Kate **Ellis**, of Hartford, Conn., **daughter of a** physician of wealth, deciding **that home** life was wearisome without something to do, learned **Shorthand and** took a position with the house of Estes & Lauriat, Boston, **Mass., at** $18 per week.

Miss Clara A. Tissington, of Nassau, Bahama Islands, on learning the art, became assistant to Mr. E. F. Underhill and other New-York law reporters. The remuneration being about double that gained by her former profession—music.

Miss Ida Stevens, of Iowa, a school teacher became stenographer to a large manufacturing house in New-York. This position was in time resigned to make a visit to her home, where the Diagonal Route Railroad Co., of Des Moines, learning that she was a stenographer, offered her a position at a better salary than she received in New-York, which she accepted.

Miss V. J. Preston, of Dutchess Co., after trying the vicissitudes of a clerkship in a dry goods store, upon graduating in Shorthand, became the chief stenographer of Ehrich Brothers, (where she was only a clerk before) at an increased salary, which position was resigned to accept a better one in the editorial sanctum of the Christian Union newspaper, and this again was given up for a still better position with Prof Phelix Adler, the Founder and President of the Society of Ethical Culture. She has here enjoyed intellectual treats rare and beautiful indeed.

Mrs. F. Wilkes, of California, the wife of a millionaire, learned the art as a precaution in case of unforeseen reverses in fortune, which was a very wise thing to do. She acknowledges that she has already derived from its study more pleasure and information than from anything else she ever undertook, and feels fully repaid for the expense of learning in intellectual benefits derived, even if she never have occasion to practise it.

Miss Amelia Tong, of Brooklyn, N. Y., a saleslady in a dry goods store, by a knowledge of the coveted art was advanced to the private secretaryship of Mr. Barnes, the head of the great publishing house of A. S. Barnes & Co., at a salary double what she received as saleslady.

Miss Lizzie Gaston, of Brooklyn, a lady of leisure learned the art to dispel the ennui of her social surroundings, became stenographer to the editor of the Christian Union at a salary that afforded her independence and pleasure.

Miss Lizzie Dolson, New Paltz, N. Y., became stenographer to the National Trotting Association of Hartford Conn., and afterward to the Custom House brokers, F. R. Downing & Co., of New-York, and finally changed to the Domestic Sewing Machine Co., for a better position. In all of which places she commanded an excellent salary, and each time she made a change it bettered her condition. Was formerly a teacher.

Miss Rena Hodges, of Mass., became stenographer to the Extensive Plate Glass house of Semon, Bache & Co, which position she resigned to accept a better one with F. R. Downing & Co., of 20 Exchange Place, New-York. Was a teacher before.

The Misses Annie A. and Kate O. Seaman, teachers of the High School of Nyack, N. Y., after four months study of the art, took positions together in Mr. L. W. Seavey's popular Scenic Art studio of New-York, where they are receiving larger remuneration than they received as school teachers.

PRICE LIST OF REPORTERS' MATERIAL.

REPORTERS' NOTE-BOOKS.

These Prices include Postage.

	EACH.	DOZEN.
No. 1 Note-Book, 4 x 9 inches, for pen, 96 pages, opening endwise, ruled for law-reporting, made for patent cover,	10 cts.	$1.20
No. 2 Note-Book, 5 x 9 inches, for pen, 160 pages, opening endwise, for office, lecture, or law reporting, made for patent cover,	20 "	2.
No. 3 Note-Book, 4 x 9 inches, for pencil, 96 pages, without marginal line,	8 "	.75
No. 4 Note-Book, 4 x 9 inches, for pencil, 192 pages, like No. 3, only double the thickness,	10 "	1.20
No. 5 Note-Book, 5 x 9 inches, medium paper for pen or pencil, 160 pages, the amanuensis' favorite book for taking dictation of business letters, also preferred for lecture or sermon reporting,	20 "	2.
No. 6 Note-Book, 5 x 9 inches, for pen, 160 pages, suitable for law, lecture or office reporting,	20 "	2.
No. 7 Note-Book, about 5 1-4 x 8 1-4 inches, medium paper for pen or pencil, opening like an ordinary book, and adapted to legal general, or office reporting,	20 "	2.
No. 8 Note-Book, 5 x 9 inches, medium paper for pen or pencil, opening endwise, ruled for law, office or general reporting, the only perfectly flexible back note-book made, bound in stiff covers, 160 pages and every sheet laying perfectly flat,	25 "	3.

---o---

REPORTERS' NOTE-BOOK COVERS.

These books are made to fit the Note-Books above described. They are useful to the Reporter, not only as a protection for the book, but as well for a stiffening or back by which the book can be held in the hand or rest upon the knee in writing. The numbers of the covers correspond to the numbers of the books to which they belong. The books are made transferable so that one cover can be used an indefinite time on different books. Nos. 1 and 2 covers are patent back, but the other covers would fit any book of the same dimensions. Order by the following numbers, 1, 2, 3, 5, 7. Price 50 cents each.

PENS, PENCILS, ETC., ETC.

The ordinary pen or pencil does not answer for shorthand writing any more than for artists' work; special pens and pencils have to be used, as follows, sent post-paid.

	DOZEN.	GROSS.
"U" PEN.—A smooth, fine pointed pen, of great durability, for longhand or shorthand writing,	20 cts.	$2.
ESTERBROOK'S FALCON.—A most excellent pen,	20 cts.	$2.
SPENCERIAN.—Especially adapted to artistic shorthand writing where a very fine line and handsome shading is required,	20 cts.	$2.
THREE POINTED PEN.—A great favorite; used entirely by the Congressional Reporters; short-nibbed, very flexible near the point, quick acting, greatly reducing the labor of writing, and lessening the tendency to Writer's Paralysis. Price,	20 cts.	$2.

Any other Pen preferred by Stenographers can be furnished to order.

	EACH.
GOLD PEN.—Short nibbed, qnick acting, made especially for shorthand writing, and after a thorough test by Stenographers pronounced the best gold pen for their uses. Selected to suit the hand of the purchaser, by his sending a sample of his longhand writing, and style of steel pen used,	$2.25
FOUNTAIN PEN.—Made for shorthand writing, coarse or fine pointed as desired, will not clog or leak, writes with any good ink, accepted by thousands of stenographers as the best, and will write a whole day with one filling. Price recently reduced one third, Plain,	$3.50
Gold mounted,	4.00
MAMMOTH PEN-HOLDER for relief to the hand in continuous writing, superior to any devise for enlarging the ordinary holder, will take any size pen, is a thing of beauty, ebonized and handsomely decorated by hand painting. Would make a unique present for any one stenographer or not.	25 cts.
CEDAR PEN-HOLDER.—Suitable for any pen, keeps the ink from soiling the fingers or the work if dropped upon the desk; without the steel ferrule which is supposed to aggravate or tend to cause writer's cramp. 6 for 25 cts. No smaller order filled unless when other goods are ordered with which it can be packed.	
PEN AND PENCIL CASE.—Carries a full set of sharpened pencils without breaking the points, Fountain, Mammoth, Gold Pen and Holder, Rubber and Steel Eraser, made durable and convenient for the pocket.	50 cts.

	EACH.	DOZEN.

PENCILS.—The best for Stenographer's use.
No. 1; pure black, without grit, and with a line of shorthand engraved on the same. - 10 cts. $1.
No. 2, with permanent rubber tips, 10 cts. $1.

CELLULOID OR HARD RUBBER PENHOLDERS; very handsome and durable, assorted colors, 10 cts. 1.

INK-ERASERS.—For typewriter use, 10 cts. 1.

PENCIL CASE.—In black or red leather, as handsome as morrocco, holding six pencils, made very strong and a sure protection to the points of pencils. $2.

POCKET INK STANDS.—Can be carried in the vest pocket, will not tip over when in use, have large mouths, and are just the thing for stenographers' use. 50 c's. $1 or $3.

LEAD PENCIL SHARPENER, a simple device convenient for the pocket, combining a knife with a file for sharpening a pencil so as to prevent waste and soiling the fingers. Price 40 cts.

STEEL POCKET ERASER.—Opens like a knife, made with a cocoa or ivory handle paper cutter for trimming books, paper, etc., etc. - - - - - - 50 cts.

TYPEWRITING PAPER.

As cheap as ordinary paper and produces the neatest effect in typewriter work. Single quire postpaid; per ream, by express.

	QUIRE.	REAM
STOCK "A", Bankers' Linen, Legal, manifolds, plain,	15c.	$1.75
STOCK "A", Letter size,	12c.	1.50
STOCK "A", Legal Cap, ruled for copying testimony,	18c.	2.00
BOND "E", Heavy, Wove, Legal, for single copies only,	25c.	2.50
IRISH LINEN, Heavy, Laid, Legal, for single copies,	25c.	2.50
ONION SKIN, Legal or letter size, Manifolds many copies,	15c.	2.50
	DOZ.	HUNDRED
CARBON, Legal Cap, best, will not smut, very durable,	60c.	5.00
COPY COVERS, for Legal matter,	15c.	75c.

CALIGRAPH AND TYPEWRITER RIBBONS.

When ordering please state for which machine the ribbon is wanted

EACH.

RECORD, for manifolding and neat jobs, black or purple, $1.
COPYING, for preservation in Letter Book, any color, 1.
INDELIBLE, Selvedge edge, giving a permanent copy any color 1.50
RIBBONS REINKED for fifty cents each.

VARIOUS CONVENIENCES.

OIL.—The only really first-class typewriter machine oil to be had.—Price 25 cents per bottle.

POCKET OIL CAN.—Neat and secure from leaking.—Price 15 cts.

TAPE OR CORD.—For use in binding typewriter copy.—Per ball or roll.—25 cents.

PAPER FASTENERS for binding copied matter,—per box of 100, ordinary size, 30 cents.

READY BINDER for business papers, reporters' notes, loose papers, letters, or periodicals, 10 cents each; 3 for 25 cents.

TYPEWRITER BRUSHES.—One for cleaning the type from ink, and the other for keeping the parts clear from dust. Price 10 cents each.

RUBBER BANDS for Typewriter, 5 cents per pair. 25 cents per half dozen pairs, assorted sizes for office use, 25 cents a dozen.

TYPEWRITER COPY HOLDER, made of metal, saves time and eyes, and adds profit to labor, sent by express at purchaser's expense.—Price $2.00.

PHONOGRAPHIC CORRESPONDENCE PAPER.—This paper is put up in neat boxes, containing one quire each with envelopes to match, ruled in red and a unique symbolical design of the art printed on the paper and envelopes, making it very stylish paper for shorthand correspondence.—Price per box, 25 cents.

COPY COVERS.—In imitation of alligator skin, very handsome for binding typewriter copied plays or general matter.—Price 10 cents each.

TYPEWRITER CABINET, black walnut, four drawers, with waste paper box, a very useful piece of furniture. Price $10.

EIGHT DRAWER CABINET, looks like an ordinary library table when the machine is not in use. When wanted the machine comes up from a recess in the desk by the aid of a spring. The handsomest and most perfect protector for any writing machine ever made. It also contains conveniences for doing the work required by the stenographer in ruling, folding papers, etc., etc., without removing the machine combining a typewriter table with an office desk, being complete to be used for either purpose or for both at the same time, without inconvenience. Price $40.

CLOTH BINDER FOR THE MONTHLY, or any magazine of the same dimensions without regard to thickness, such as the Century St. Nicholas, etc., etc. So simple it is understood when first seen. Price 75 cents.

TYPEWRITERS.—Any make of machine for Stenographers' use will be supplied from this office at the lowest price at which the machines can be sold by any agent. On some machines the agent's prices can be discounted.

EYE SHADE for protection for the eyes in working by artificial light, made of cloth and perforated for ventilation, of an agreeable instead of sore-eye color. Price 15 cents each.

HAND-BAG, with compartments for carrying notes, transcripts, legal or other papers, having a handle, lock, chain or strap to hang from the shoulder if desired. Indispensable to lady stenographers, as it serves every purpose of a pocket and is more secure and commodious. Price $2 and $4. The cheaper ones being without lock or shoulder strap.

THE NEW PEN-HOLDER gives to any steel pen the flexibility and ease of a gold pen, holding a pen with any degree of firmness desired. The freedom of action that is allowed to the shank of a pen within this pen-holder removes entirely the feeling of rigidity and stiffness, and consequent strain upon the muscles of the fingers and wrist that accompanies the use of all ordinary pen-holders, thereby making this one thoroughly anti-nervous; accommodates itself to any pen, and the flexibility of the pen can be changed by turning the screw-head in the holder; made of rubber and very durable. Price 25 cents. Mammoth size 40 cents. Pocket Reverse Holder, 55 cts.

OTHER SUPPLIES which may come into the market from time to time, will be furnished from this office; in fact, anything the student or stenographer needs or which may be helpful to him in any way, can be had from us whether it is found on our present list or not. So please send us your order for whatever you may want and be assured that by our prompt and fair dealing we will deserve your continued patronage.

www.ingramcontent.com/pod-product-compliance
Lightning Source LLC
Chambersburg PA
CBHW030403170426
43202CB00010B/1469